Delving Further B

Rev Neville Barker Cryer

First published 2009

ISBN 978 0 85318 319 8

Published by Lewis Masonic

an imprint of Ian Allan Publishing Ltd,
Hersham, Surrey KT12 4RG.
Printed by Ian Allan Printing Ltd,
Hersham, Surrey KT12 4RG

Code: 0904/A2

Visit the Lewis Masonic website at www.lewismasonic.com

Contents

Introduction

This book may seem to have a somewhat strange title. However that may strike you, there are two things that have to be made clear at the outset of this work. The first is that what is offered here is in no way meant as a replacement for the work *Beyond the Craft* by Brother Keith Jackson, nor, secondly, is it meant to be in any way some sort of criticism of that work. The numbers and extent of past and present readers of that book are testimony enough to its having met, and to its continuing to meet, an evident desire for Masonic clarification. It is a reference book that has clearly been highly effective in providing information for many brethren about what are the other branches of English Freemasonry that are around, apart from the Craft and the Holy Royal Arch, and what one has to do to take part in them. What the book's appearance revealed was the widespread interest that many had in the many and varied parts of our Freemasonry and even in those parts that they may never be able to join. *Beyond the Craft* was, is, and will continue to be, an essential handbook for the whole of the foreseeable future.

It is, indeed, just because that book has been so successful that there has arisen, as a direct result, a perception by many of its readers that there was surely still more of interest and value to be uncovered about the more detailed origin of all those Orders and degrees that Brother Jackson so usefully introduced. More recently I have myself been asked if I would write papers on the origins of some degrees, and it is the updated or further researched versions of such papers that have provided part of what follows.

In deference to the devoted work of other authors it has to be admitted that there are several individual histories of some of the Orders dealt with here, and a list of these is included in a 'Further Reading' section of this book. However, the main difference between what is in those books and the information provided here is that they properly record the whole story of their subject, from a known origin up to the time of the degree's development and management at the date when their work was published, whereas the chapters in this book will deal solely with the roots from which each of the branches of Freemasonry that are here selected grew and will stop at a point where that branch assumed a shape with which we are familiar today. It is about these roots that a growing number of enquirers are both curious and intrigued to learn. The detailed story of these beginnings is just what was not planned to be provided in *Beyond the Craft* and that is the gap that it is now intended to plug.

It is also necessary to point out that in certain of the topics dealt with here the Order being examined will have distinctive elements within it that need special, individual attention. This is seen particularly in the case of the Allied Degrees, which are themselves a collection of varied Masonic practices with their own quite separate derivations. It may, therefore, be a matter of especial interest to discover the roots of the degree of St. Lawrence or the proper place of the Order of the Grand High Priest. The same is true of the Order of the Red Cross of Constantine in which two additional grades have a history all their own. Whilst when we come to the components of the Holy Royal Arch Knight Templar Priests we have an even more diverse set of practices to consider.

It is this more detailed attention to what are some of the comprehensive Masonic practices included here that explains why this book does not deal with all those Masonic branches that are included in Brother Jackson's book. It may, of course, soon catch your attention that there is no inclusion here of the Order of the Holy Royal Arch. That is because the next book that this author is planning to produce will be entitled *The Royal Arch Journey: Its Sources and Early Development up to 1834*. Even to have attempted to deal with that subject here would have resulted in a huge imbalance in the contents. In any case the chapters in this book are necessarily longer and also more detailed than in Bro. Jackson's work, at least as far as history is concerned, and so a further book providing for the rest of all his material will be considered in the light of how this work is received. To this end both the publishers and the author will appreciate comments from readers on what is provided here. If there is sufficient interest, a second set of 'origins' will be produced.

There are two general features connected with the degrees in *Beyond the Craft* that are dealt with here which need a mention so that they are not repeatedly explained. Several of what are now separate degrees were once practised as part of the larger Craft in pre-Union days, at least in Antients or Antients-style lodges. Accordingly those parts of Masonry did not have, because they did not need, ceremonies of opening and closing or special rites for the Installation of rulers since these functions were already provided in their 'parent' lodge or chapter. In the traditional working of the Grand Lodge of All England at York there never was a separate Opening ritual for the Apprentice Degree; even in the 1770s it was urged that the old practice of conferring the grade of Apprentice in the Fellows lodge was changed and an Apprentice was initiated separately. Even today most of the intermediate degrees of the Ancient and Accepted Rite or the subsidiary degrees of the Holy Royal Arch Knight Templar Priests do not have these additional ceremonies.

The same development also explains why, when a ceremony no longer took place as part of the Craft, there was a need for other varied forms of dress. It should not surprise the reader, therefore, in examining the earliest forms of the degrees, if it seems as though these aspects have been overlooked. It is just that new regalia was only later required as earlier connections were discontinued.

The second point is even more general but no less important. In outlining the development of degrees we have to keep in mind the difference between the form of the lodge, a chapter or conclave, and the content of the ritual or ceremony that was conducted in, or distinguished by, that form. This becomes apparent when we have what is called a Mark lodge but what takes place there is either noticeably different from another such lodge of the same name or is a ceremony that appears in another unit with a quite different name. Both these variations have to be taken into account in what follows.

It only remains to thank those who have made this work possible. Much is owed to those already referred to who have written the longer works about some of the Degrees mentioned, the authors of a century and more ago who took the trouble to record the early developments of what were then new Degrees and Orders, the librarians and curators who have made available some works that reveal the small, hidden but vital elements in some of these practices that could so easily be overlooked or forgotten, and not least Brother Jackson's book itself which is the reason and basis for this presentation.

If, supplied with all this valuable assistance, the final conclusions that are offered in the pages that follow differ on occasions from those of my predecessors then it is on me and not them that any judgement, favourable or otherwise, must fall. This author has sought to reach the most complete solutions that the available evidence could indicate. All that I now hope is that armed with this work and its predecessor the Freemason of the future will not only be aware of what is available for him to join but will value the historical traditions to be found in their origin and working. It is a very rich, rewarding and fascinating field of study.

The Mark Masonry Trail

An interest in working masons' marks has, it would seem, been a regular feature of both the research and the talks that have occupied Masonic brethren for the last century and a half. The interest is a legitimate one, not only because of its fascination as a study but because the idea of the 'mark' has been a distinctive and continuing element in Mark Masonic ritual. It is obviously the reason for retaining 'Mark' as the name of the degree, or, as we ought perhaps more properly still to say, the Mark degrees.

That operative stonemasons were provided with a personal and distinctive mark for use on a working site is undoubted and in some situations this mark was adopted by descendants of the original craftsman to whom it had been given. It was this practice of identifying a fellow with an indented mark on the stones he fashioned that was transferred into Accepted Freemasonry, as revealed by the 17th century register of the principal Lodge in Aberdeen. There, side by side, are the approved marks of operative and non-operative brethren. Exactly the same practice is known to have been the case a century or more later in the Mark Book of St. John of Jerusalem Lodge No.8, in Redruth, Cornwall.

This evidence of Masons being made 'Mark Men' by the registration of their personal mark was not, however, the whole of the early Mark story. In addition to receiving a mark there was also the presence of catechisms or lectures in 17th and 18th century Lodges and in these, as in those customary in the Grand Lodge of All England at York, there was an explanation of the marks applied by the overseers to certify the quality of the craftsmanship, as well as that of the master mason that gave an indication as to where and how a stone was to be laid. The lectures also began to relate the stories of the mislaid keystone or an undervalued cornerstone with all its biblical associations. In the increasingly established context of the story of the building of Solomon's Temple, or of its successor after the return from the exile in Babylon, such stories had an even more recognisable significance. The common practice of presenting explanatory lectures to the seated candidate, after he had taken his obligation and been clothed with an apron, is often overlooked in the search for the origins of our degrees. We are so used to the idea of a degree as an almost entirely acted event that to talk of a degree being in existence when it consisted mainly of lectures providing an explanation or interpretation is not easy to grasp. Expecting and looking for an acted event has been the case especially for the last 200 years, following the 1813 Union of Grand Lodges, when the use of catechetical lectures was widely discontinued. It is only recently that the value of explanatory commentary has begun to be appreciated afresh.

What this means is that if we are seeking to find the source of some degree it is not enough to give up the search when we at last apparently discover something that looks like what we take for granted as a Mark or other degree ceremony. That is why what Dunckerley presented to his Chapter companions in Portsmouth in 1769 is not the start of our story. Quite apart from his own presumably honest declaration to them that he had 'RECENTLY received' the Mark elsewhere it is now known that in at least Newcastle, Gateshead, Sunderland and Durham, not to mention other parts of the country, a recognisably Mark activity was already in place. This is not, of course, to say that such activity was the same in each place, and Dunckerley may well have added special touches of his own. Creating a two-stage form of Mark practice, the degrees of Mark Man and Mark Master, may well have been his particular contribution. What we have to recognise is that where a Mark element is present in local Masonic practice up to this point it was acknowledged as part and parcel of Craft working, and to repeat what has just been said, that meant it was part of catechetical instruction round a table. In *The Arch and the Rainbow* I have given examples of how that was being done in Ireland by the middle of the 18th century.

There are two other factors that have to be recognised. The first is that by 1759 the Grand Secretary of the premier Grand Lodge, otherwise known as that of the Moderns, showed in a remark made to an Irish Mason that he was aware of a form of Freemasonry known as The Arch Degree. We now know that this was what is now called the Most Excellent Master Degree, the purpose of which was to represent the act that signalled the completion of the building of Solomon's Temple by the recovered keystone being carried in a formal procession and it then being set in its proper place as the cape or headstone of the arched doorway to the Holy of Holies. This ceremony is today practised as one of the ceremonies in the series of the Royal and Select Masters, or Cryptic degrees, and it is also named in a list of appendant degrees attached to the Order of Holy Royal Arch Knight Templar Priests. In this latter list it is placed before the Excellent Master or Veils degree which is exactly where the Mark degree comes in Scotland. There cannot be any doubt that this ceremony indicated the presence of the Mark theme in English 18th century Freemasonry and especially its connection with both the Craft and the Holy Royal Arch. It is a further clue as to why Dunckerley chose a Royal Arch occasion for his introduction of the Mark to his Moderns brethren.

The other factor revealing an early relationship between the Mark theme and ancient Craft Masonry is shown in the form of ceremony then called the Heredom of Kilwinning that was being worked in London in the late 1730s at least. Almost the whole of the ritual used in this form of Masonry is catechetical and in verse, and close to the start of the ceremony we have this:

Q. What in Masonry is said to represent the Son of Man?
A. The perpend-ashlar.
Q. What is the perpend-ashlar called besides?
A. The Stone that the Builders rejected, which is now become the Chief Stone of the Corner, or the most perfect pattern for Masons to try their Moral Jewels upon.
Q. In what is it said to be the most perfect pattern?
A. In the three great principles of Masonry.
Q. What are they?
A. Brotherly Love, Relief and Truth.

What this means is that the Mark aspect of Freemasonry was inherent from the very beginning of Accepted ritual, a fact that is embodied in the very words we use at the obligation as we vow not to 'mark, cut, carve, indite or engrave'. How that Mark aspect of our work was expressed was, of course, a different matter. It is highly revealing to note that when, in Scotland, as the 19th century began, the decision was made by the Grand Lodge there to exclude the ritual bestowing of marks and recovery of the keystone as part of Craft Masonry there was opposition from a number of lodges, though by no means all of them, because those lodges claimed that making Mark Masons had been part of their local practice from Time Immemorial. It was as a result of that contention that a form of Mark ceremony was still to be allowed to be conferred in such Craft lodges as desired it.

Exactly the same situation existed in England and at the same period, but when at the Union the decision was reached to limit the practice of Ancient Masonry to three degrees and the Order of the Holy Royal Arch no similar contention or request by any local lodges to retain their Mark usage seems to have been made, and those that practised Mark ceremonies seem to have simply continued their pre-Union custom, in their own peculiar fashion and form. This situation continued until some rightly zealous new Provincial Grand Masters required of such lodges that either they should end these Mark Mason practices altogether or arrange for them to be performed on an evening other than a Craft lodge occasion. Not only did this latter happen but the styles of Mark Masonry that then developed showed the signs of their distinctive and separate origins. As one who has had access to the oldest known forms of worked Mark degrees, as opposed to the earliest lecture forms, of this period, I have to record that what has been published recently of those Mark forms was a deliberately chosen common denominator of late 18th and early 19th century ceremonies and there could in fact have been many other incidental variations if one had included all the information to hand.

It was, indeed, the sheer variety and individuality of the workings in those lodges that continued the Mark tradition that probably led eventually to the desire for a more fixed and authoritative style of Mark Masonry such as that which was practised in Scotland. What is also notable is that when some fairly influential and high ranking English Masons met an enthusiastic and knowledgeable Mark Master Mason from north of the border at the 1851 Great Exhibition in London it did not deter them when they discovered that he represented the Mark practice as authorised by the Grand Chapter of Scotland and not that of the Craft lodges in that land. This was to be a move that had serious implications for the future relations between the duly authorised 'Scottish' Mark Masons in England and those existing English Masons who had their established Mark degree attachments.

Such variation certainly cannot have been a helpful guide to those Masons who were charged by the United Grand Lodge of England to experience a Mark ceremony and report back as to whether this was a proper adjunct to the Craft in its post-Union situation. There is no known, or at least no certain, reason why an initially favourable opinion of the Mark degree was deleted from the Grand Lodge minutes, but a number of uncertainties that attended the Mark in those mid-19th century days could have been ample reason for an unwillingness to disturb the progress of a new Craft Masonry in England. If there were any English Masons who wished to be holders of a Mark degree then it was now clear that they would have to devise their own means for achieving that goal. The fact that there were several varied forms of Mark custom around was to be not the least of their problems.

It is thus that we come to the last stages of our Mark Masonic journey in

England. Rejected as part of the normal Craft life of English brethren there was only one solution – there would have to be a separate governing body for the Mark and that body would have to gain the allegiance of both the older English units that practised a Mark ceremony and the newer Mark units that owed their existence to a Scottish tradition and rule, just when the Grand Chapter of Scotland was increasingly anxious not to make difficulties for a sister body, the Supreme Grand Chapter of England.

A new decision had likewise to be made in regard to the appointment of officers. Bearing in mind the distinctive feature of the Mark degrees which entailed the checking, and – if approved – the marking, of such work, there needed to be some who acted as Overseers. In some earlier forms of Mark practice the Worshipful Master, Senior and Junior Wardens doubled up as Overseers for part of the proceedings, but other old lodges had introduced three separate appointments and this was the system that was eventually adopted. This was also important for the new Opening and Closing procedures which became necessary when the Mark ceremony could not any more be given as part of Craft practice. Having the new Master, Senior and Junior Overseers explaining their duties when the lodge opened, or surrendering their plans at the closing, gave a distinctive touch to what might otherwise have been just a very similar Craft occasion.

In the post-Union era it was necessary for each degree to have its own clothing, and several different designs were tried before the present form was adopted. The similarity of not only the basic apron but also those of Provincial and Grand Officers with those in the Craft, albeit subtly mixing the Craft and Chapter colours, has proved to be successful and has suggested the link with the old elements of Masonry that were rejected as formal attachment in 1851.

Finally, the Mark Grand Lodge, after much deliberation, decided on a moderate revision of two older tracing boards that had been in circulation to accompany the earlier forms of Mark ceremony. Today the tracing board occupies an honourable place among the lodge furniture, but – as with the Cipher alphabet – singularly little explanation of these two items is often given.

These matters having been settled, the Mark Masters degree in England acquired those characteristics with which its members are still familiar. They are characteristics that are peculiar to English Mark Masonry and its various daughter branches across the world. It now has a tradition of 150 years, but, as we have seen, that tradition emerged from a very much older ancestry that was recognised in England, Ireland and Scotland as early as the start of Accepted Freemasonry in the late 16th and early 17th centuries. The fact that it took so long for what we enjoy today to emerge should not disguise the fact that the Mark tradition is one that forms 'a graceful addition' to our Craft experience and ought truly to be regarded as a necessary part of being a complete Freemason.

Uncovering the Origins of the Ark Mariner Degree

In view of the host of Masonic studies in the last 120 years it is surprising how little has been written on the Ark Mariner degree. Considering the known antiquity of the Noah theme that underlies this Masonic practice it is further surprising that so little attention has been paid to it. It should be mentioned here that Ark Mariner lodges in the USA are referred to in this book in the chapter on the Order of the Secret Monitor (see pp24, 26)

Brother Keith Jackson tells us that whilst there is some doubt as to the reliability of the claim that in 1772 a Grand Lodge of the Ark Mariners was reconstituted, 'the first authentic record of the degree appears in the minutes of a meeting held in Bath in 1790' (op. cit. p.18). What this assertion is based on is an extract from a document called the Purday Manuscript of 1861 which reads as follows:

Royal Ark Lodge or the (Pillar) of an Ark Mason
Laid open in the form of a lecture as handed down from Noah to
the present time and carefully transcribed from Ancient Records
by Ebenezer Sibly DGN [Deputy Grand Noah] 1790.

The ceremony that follows consists of a long address, handing over of tools, and a catechetical lecture. The whole of this is reproduced in my book, *The Arch and the Rainbow* (pp.382-3). One recent lecturer has, on this basis, suggested that 'Noah' Sibly, as he was known, was so enthusiastic as to fabricate the degree, though the lecturer goes on to admit as another possibility that 'Sibly adapted a far older degree, perhaps as in Ark, Mark, Link and Wrestle, elaborated it and brought it up to date'. In view of the significant words appearing on the title page above, 'carefully transcribed from Ancient Records', I would suggest that this latter judgement is the one that is more correct.

Whilst the Sibly creation is verifiable evidence, it has to be pointed out that this is referring to an occasion when the story of Noah, his family, the deluge and the rainbow were being picked out as incidents for separate presentation when previously such events would have been known and recited as part of the basic degrees in the ancient Craft. If we are to discover the true ancestry of the quite modest degree that is enjoyed today it is to a time rather further back that we shall have to go.

The above reference can prove there were Ark lodges already in existence before 1790, but what was more significant was that they owed their existence to the emergence of an Early Grand Scottish Rite of forty-four degrees which, in its turn, was derived from the Early Grand Encampment of 1765 in Ireland. Already we can see that the ancestry of the Ark Mariner strain is much older than often imagined. As Brother Keith Jackson also points out, a Brother John Darrington sought to revive interest in the Ark Mariner in 1816. When the descendants of those Freemasons who had assisted him were ready to hand over this degree to the rulers of the Grand Mark Lodge, they made what was by some thought to be the excessive claim that an Ark Mariner tradition was already more than 200 years old. That would have taken the degree back to the 1670s, so if even what has just been proposed in regard to Irish origins is correct then the claim would seen to have been astonishingly excessive. But can it nonetheless be true?

There are signs in a Stirling lodge that suggest that by the mid-1740s there was awareness of other degrees, including the Ark Mariner (see pp80, 81). Retreating another decade, in the Royal Order of Scotland ceremony – then called the Heredom of Kilwinning – there are elements of Masonic ritual that are almost unchanged from the late 1730s, and an extract from the Heredom's working is as follows:

What was the first building under divine direction?
Noah's ark.
To what intent was it built?
To preserve the elect from the deluge.
How many persons were there preserved?
Eight: four men and four women.
Name the men.
Noah, Japhet, Shem and Ham, all masons true.
[and shortly after]
What ought Freemasons chiefly to commemorate?
Three great events – The Creation of the World, Noah's Flood and the Redemption of Man.
To what intent?
The Glory of God.

Nor is that all. If we consider the authorised Constitutions of the premier Grand Lodge inaugurated in 1717 we find that their first appearance in 1720 has due notice of Noah and the Flood. What has to be specially noted here is that these 'Old Constitutions' are claimed to have been 'Taken from a Manuscript wrote (sic) above Five Hundred Years since'. That would take the contents back to 1220, so if anyone has any doubts about the antiquity of some of the Noah's Ark traditions this set of the 'Old Constitutions' seems to answer them. What we read here is:

'You ask me how this Science was invented: my Answer is this. That before the General Deluge, which is commonly called Noah's Flood [that being the name constantly used for a section of the Mystery plays from about 1370] there was a man called Lamech … [whose] four Children found the beginning of all Crafts in the World … [and] they did write these Sciences, that they had found, on two Pillars of Stone, that they might be found after that GOD had taken Vengeance for Sins … that would not drown in Water … It resteth now to tell you how these stones were found … after the said Deluge: It so pleased God Almighty, that the great Hermamermes [sic] … who was the Son of Sem [sic], who was the Son of Noah. The said Hermarmes was afterwards called Hermes [and] he found one of the 2 Pillars of Stone. He found these Sciences written thereon, and taught them to other Men.'

It is thus that Noah begins to play his part in the preservation of what our form of Masonry was to teach. In the Grand Lodge's commissioned edition of 1723, the author, the Reverend Dr. Anderson, includes in the appointed Address to a new Brother the following passages:

'…at length NOAH, the ninth from Seth (one of Adam's sons), was commanded and directed of God to build the great Ark which, tho' of Wood, was certainly fabricated by Geometry, and according to the Rules of Masonry. NOAH, and his three Sons, JAPHET, SHEM and HAM all Masons true, brought with them over the Flood the Traditions and Arts of the Ante-diluvians and amply communicated them to their growing Offspring: for about 101 Years after the Flood, we find a vast Number of 'em, if not the whole Race of Noah, in the Vale of Shinar, employ'd in building a City and large Tower, in order to make to themselves a Name…'

What is worth emphasising here is that from what Anderson called the 'Faithful Traditions of many Ages', and at the outset of what we can call this more lasting form of Accepted Freemasonry, the Noah, or Noachic, element in English Masonry was firmly signalled. It came from an earlier strain of ceremonial practice and this was in fact underlined by what was included in further editions of the Constitutions in 1726, 1730 and 1738. In the 1726 edition we read 'That before the Generall Deluge, which is commonly called Noah's Flood, there was a Man called Lamech' whose children, including Tubal-Cain, sought to preserve the Sciences as we learnt earlier. Mention is also made there of Hermes Trismagistus whom 'some think to be Grandson to Cush, which was grandson to Noah'. Clearly the Noachic theme cannot be avoided and, moreover, in the Pennell or Irish 1730 edition of the Constitutions a passage on the building of the Ark is very similar to that of 1723, but we are also told that 'it was a wonderful Piece of Geometrical Masonry, whereby they saved themselves and their Wives from the Flood. The tower in the valley of Shinar is named Babel'.

What is striking about this Pennell edition of the Constitutions is the extended mention of the influence of the descendants of Noah's sons. 'Mizraim, the second son of Ham, brought the Royal Art of Masonry into Egypt, about six years after the confusion of Babel, and 160 after the Flood.' This explains why, in Victorian times, there would be an attempt to introduce a form of Masonry called the Order of Mizraim.

The Pennell edition continues:

'And surely the fair and gallant Posterity of Japhet [the eldest son of Noah] such as travelled into the Isles of the Gentiles, must have been equally skill'd in Geometry and Masonry… [whilst] …The Posterity of Shem was not unskilful in the Learned Arts. This select Family long used Military Architecture...'

It is this document that makes a great deal of the old Tower of Babel as it speaks at length of the subsequent exile in Babylon and the exit therefrom.

When we come to the Anderson revision of 1738, what he writes is this: 'Noachidae, or Sons of Noah, was the first name of Masons, according to some old Traditions'. He also introduces that term into the first of the Old Charges, so that 'A Mason is obliged by his Tenure to observe the Moral Law, as a true Noachida', and later in that same Charge he speaks of the 'Three Great Articles of Noah'.

This early English identification of a Noachic element in Masonic tradition and instruction is further strengthened by the story in the Graham Manuscript. This document has mostly been accepted as dating from 1726, though some suggest it is from 1672 (this latter date accords with what has been admitted as the style of handwriting in the original manuscript). Certainly it must have been used in some Masonic circles some time before it was recorded in a document. Accordingly it can be recognised that around the start of the 18th century, or earlier, we have a remarkably similar story to the more familiar one of the discovery of the body of Hiram Abiff, but in this case the subject is Noah who is found and raised by his three sons. If it was this event to which the eventual 19th century transmitters of an Ark practice were referring then they were not making such an exaggerated claim as may have been thought.

If, as thus appears to be the case, there was a Noah strand in at least some presentations of the early Free and Accepted Masonic catechisms or lectures, the question may properly be put as to why this aspect did not persist into the premier, and then the Antients, Grand Lodge era.

One answer may be that despite the apparently logical place of Noah and the Ark within the story of how Accepted Freemasonry arose, this emphasis carried with it too many medieval or Catholic implications for the newly enlightened men of post-1717. There was no doubt that the salvation of mankind by the Messiah story was paralleled in the Middle Ages by the Noah event. The dynastic connection mentioned earlier between Shem and Jesus Christ, the symbolic salvation by water of God's people as a direct reference to the sacrament of baptism, and the Ark, as a ship for God's chosen people, being the origin of part of a Christian church being called a nave (from the Latin word, 'navis', a ship) all support such a theory. When to this you add a story of Noah being roused from taking too much wine you have an intimation of another sacrament, and the link of the Noah incident with medieval teaching is complete.

It is hardly surprising that as the constructors of the premier Grand Lodge government included a fair number of men who were members of the Huguenot, Presbyterian and anti-Jacobite persuasions, they thought Hiram Abiff should replace such a partisan figure as Noah must have seemed. That said, it is even less surprising, given the part that Noah had earlier been seen to have played in the development of Accepted Freemasonry, that there were many brethren who were eager to preserve some practice of a Noachic kind. It may be a surprise for many to discover how ancient a Noah degree's ancestry may be. What is encouraging is that, despite its bumpy history, it is now once more a legitimate and appreciated part of the English Masonic scene.

The Roots of the Secret Monitor Degrees

'While the first references to the Order of David and Jonathan are known to be of Dutch origin, the Secret Monitor arose in America as a side degree conferred by any mason who had received it himself. It was brought to England by Dr. I. Zacharie when he returned from America around 1875.' That is what we are told about the early beginnings of this portion of Freemasonry by Brother Keith Jackson in *Beyond the Craft*; a simple, straightforward explanation, but it leaves several important questions unanswered.

It was in 1907, in what was a first survey of the Order by Brother W.J. Spratling, that the earliest suggestion of a possible Dutch origin for this degree occurs. This suggestion was repeated in the more comprehensive history of 1950 supplied by Dr. Henry Bayon – he added some information that implied a secret system of recognition adopted by those who were in rebellion in the Netherlands, first against the Spanish rulers of the 16th century and then against the French a century later. Certainly the close bond that was reported in the Bible to exist between the Jewish figures of David and Jonathan and their plan to communicate by secret means would seem to fit the activities of those citizens who might have sought to combine in resisting foreign oppressors.

I must point out, however, that verifiable evidence to support these interesting suggestions is not apparent and in any case even these movements seem unlikely to be related to a continental Masonry developing after 1720. In a paper given in Manchester in 1970, the then Deputy Grand Supreme Ruler, Right Worshipful Arthur Murphy, reported that the (unnamed) Librarian of the Grand East of the Netherlands thought these stories very doubtful.

In his 1964 *History of the Order of the Secret Monitor*, Colonel R.J. Wilkinson, the then Grand Librarian at Mark Masons Hall, states that an American writer of c.1880 claimed that an Order of Jonathan and David had been taken to New Amsterdam (modern-day New York) by Dutch settlers in the 17th century – sadly he does not name the 1880s American writer. This suggestion might seem at first a reasonable one – Wilkinson also mentions that according to a reference in the then-current Jewish Encyclopaedia some Dutch Jews were introducing various Masonic degrees at Newport, Rhode Island, in 1658. Unfortunately, this information has been proven totally incorrect – if we go to the latest edition of the Jewish Encyclopaedia (2004) the date given for this Newport establishment is 1780, more than a century later. In view of the generally accepted dates for the development of any separate or appendant degrees, the 1780 date would seem much more likely.

The 1964 History of this Order, however, offers two other trails of investigation. The first starts with a reference to a catalogue originally said to be in the Bibliothèque Nationale in Paris, which mentions a 1762 work titled *Abrégé des Lois et Constitutions de la Providence Divine*. In 1964, this book could not be found in the Paris collection, nor has it been found since, but its existence at least shows that the story of Jonathan and David was in circulation in the 1760s as a Masonic theme. Indeed, Brother Murphy also revealed that in 1744 there was a lodge in Brunswick in which there was a medal called 'Jonathan of the pillar' that showed Jonathan embracing David. So prominently does Solomon figure in the 1720s English Constitutional histories that we forget that it is there recorded that 'the same King David loved Masons, and cherished them… and he gave them Charges'. It would not be surprising if the tale of David with Jonathan did occur in some early lectures.

What is fact is that that French work had been the source for yet another book, written in Dutch, that appeared in 1773. This was entitled *The Rules, Statutes, Constitutions and Ceremonials of the Order of Jonathan and David and Jesus Christ*, and an original copy of this is now in the library of the Grand East (or headquarters) of Netherlands Freemasonry at The Hague. Wilkinson says that a photostat copy was given to the library of Mark Masons Hall, London, but the current archivist told me that it is no longer there. However, the Grand East Librarian kindly provided a copy for use in preparing this book and that copy will be duly lodged, like its predecessor, in London. A translation of it is also planned.

It is this book that seems to have inspired a certain Hendrik Bolt, Worshipful Master of the Lodge Concordia Vincit Animos that met in Amsterdam, to introduce this Order to his members. It is relevant to note here that this is a lodge that had obtained its Charter from the Grand Lodge of Scotland in 1755 and may thus have kept in touch with contemporary Masonic developments in that country. The significance of such a connection is that, as will become clear later, a form of this degree was being practised in Scotland from the 1770s at least. What is certainly very striking is the next action of Worshipful Brother Bolt.

For some reason, either to acquire more authority or to gain more credence for the practice, Brother Bolt applied for a Charter of Confirmation from a Roman Catholic body in Avignon that may very well have belonged to the Jesuit Order. The Charter was issued in 1788 and begins with the words:

> We, the Grand Masters Plenipotentiary of the Fraternal and Confederated Order of Jonathan and David and Jesus Christ in the name of, and under the auspices and mysterious indulgences of, His Holiness Pius [V], Sovereign Pontiff, Supreme and Ecumenical Master, Servant of the Servants of God, by the Divine Clemency, Health and Friendship to the Very Venerable Brother Knights and Friends of the said Order...

The Charter went on to say that as this Order had in recent centuries fallen into error and desuetude, New Rules, Statutes and Ceremonials were now conferred and with these Hendrik Bolt was empowered to open a Grand Chapter and confer the seven degrees of the Order. What seems perfectly clear from this declaration is that though a similar Order had been in existence earlier, its control had been in unsteady hands. The Roman Catholic authorities now regarded the Order as very much in need of reorganisation, and of being placed under their jurisdiction.

It may be helpful at this point to touch upon something of the prevailing mood within Roman Catholicism at the time. The common understanding has been that with the issue of a series of Papal Bulls after 1738, Catholics were forbidden from joining or associating with Freemasonry. This would seem to make approval or authorisation of a Masonic Order an impossibility, unless the Catholic Church had the Order under its control. It seems to be the case that during the period in question the Roman Catholic Church was trying to regain authority over at least some parts of continental Freemasonry. The Stuart pretenders to the English throne were no longer able, if they ever were, to assist in this objective.

Reverting to the matter of degrees in the Order for which Hendrik Bolt sought approval, the ones named in the 1773 Dutch publication were:

1. Squire, or Friend of the Order;
2. Knight, or Nephew;
3. Commander, or Brother;
4. Grand Commander of Jonathan and David and Knight of the Order of Jesus Christ;
5. Commander of the Order of Jesus Christ;

6. Grand Knight;

7. Grand Commander.

Brother Wilkinson claims that the rituals recorded in the first three of these degrees show clearly that 'they are an ancestral form of the modern ritual of the O.S.M.' Whilst I agree that there are portions of the first three rituals that are reminiscent of features in our form of the Order, I cannot agree with his employing the term 'ancestral' if this implies that here we have the sure, proven 'ancestor' of our present usage. In the Dutch Order the candidate was seated and listened to portions of the 14th to 23rd chapters of the First Book of Samuel. After obligation and investiture in each degree a candidate was further treated to a catechismal explanation of the objects, signs, etc, as given in an exchange between two members of the Chapter. A quote here may give us a flavour of what is a very extensive and detailed whole:

Friend: Are you in the Order of the Covenant of Jonathan and David?

Yes, Brother Director of Ceremonies.

What are you in this Order?

A Squire (or Shield-bearer).

Why do you desire to enter this Order?

That I might find myself introduced to learning what is required for human sociability.

Anything else?

Yes. I thought by doing this I would also find friendship in time of need unlike anything found elsewhere.

[The proofs of his having been properly admitted are then rehearsed and explained.]

Catechism of the 2nd Degree in Chapter Brother Knight & Nephew:

Are you in the pact of the princes Jonathan and David?

Yes, Sir Brother.

What are you in the Order?

Knight, Nephew and Companion.

Why a Knight?

Because both Jonathan and David, as inaugurators of this pact, were Princes and Generals, so it is only proper that this pact should be divided and seen as a Knightly Order.

Why a Nephew?

Because Jonathan and David, being forsworn Brothers, like us all, we being their successors, had offspring for their brothers' and sisters' children.

[There then follow the meanings of the words, grips and signs]

Catechism of the 3rd Degree in the Chapter:

Brother, are you in the Royal Covenant of the princes David and Jonathan?

Yes, Sir Brother Chancellor.

What are you in this Princely Pact of our noble Order?

Grand Knight Commander, Grand Crossbearer and covenanted Brother.

Why a Grand Knight Commander?

Because at the time of the institution and confirmed restoration [of the monarchy], Jonathan and David were both Princes under King Saul and military officials in the Forces, who had a share in, and direction of, the royal and worldly regiment as Commanders and hence there is this grand and superior grade of knighthood in this covenant Order.

Why are you covenant Brothers?

Because Jonathan and David, as privately related sons of King Saul, were Brothers. And this Covenant Order being so properly established, my membership in the Order has bound me heart and soul with my fellow brethren.

What were the reasons that led you to get involved?

Love of the Order and the Covenant, to expand one's knowledge, and if at any time my fellow brethren might be in need, to help them to the best of my ability, to offer them my hand and protection.

These extracts are surely sufficient to show the similarity, if not the exact identity, of this earlier working, with what we have today.

The 4th to the 7th degrees, which, like what preceded them, required a candidate who professed belief in the Holy Trinity, were worked in a 'Venerable Chapter' which was simply declared open but only held in the presence of the Past Grand Masters and Chancellors. The 4th degree ritual, says Brother Wilkinson, has 'references to Freemasonry in general, and to the Rose Croix'. To try and discover what he meant about 'Freemasonry in general' I had to go back to the original and it may be that the following extract may suggest what was in his mind. Quite what this had to do with the issue of the ancestry of the Order of the Secret Monitor I am far from certain. Let us, however, consider just one more portion of the Dutch Order:

These are the mysterious questions and answers relating to the Grand Principles of the 4th Degree of the Order of Jonathan and David, or of the Venerable Chapter of JC [Jesus Christ]:

What do you understand or grasp by the number 3?

1. The threefold bond of Jonathan, David and Jesus Christ, and the threefold bond between Christ with God and Man.

2. The make-up of human beings: body, spirit and soul.

3. The three witnesses in heaven: Father, Word and Spirit. The three witnesses on earth: Spirit, water and blood.

4. The three steps in Christ's humbling: birth, death and burial; the three steps of his raising: resurrection, ascension and last judgement.

5. The first three grades of the Order and their pillars: faith, love and hope.

[There then follows sections on the numbers 5 and 7, all equally couched in orthodox Christian teaching.]

In the historical catechism attached to the 5th degree, references to the Templars, Hospitallers and Knights of the Holy Sepulchre are made, but in taking this degree the candidate had to swear not only to preserve its secrets but never to reveal where and by whom he had been accepted and certainly not the names of his superiors. The 6th and 7th degrees appear to have been merely honorary.

The traditional history of this form of the Order of Jonathan and David and Jesus Christ claims that it dates back to 288CE and commemorates the work of the brothers Cosmas and Damian, two Christian Arab physicians who were martyred during the persecutions under the Roman Emperor Diocletian. The traditional narrative continues by saying that the Order was to suffer many variations of fortune and was often on the point of extinction but was always rescued by being taken under the patronage of some prominent person. It was claimed that the Order had consistently maintained a branch in England from the 12th to the 17th centuries and that during Oliver Cromwell's rule it served as a form of secret society devoted to the restoration of the Stuart royal line. Such a claim reveals the wider origin of the Order and would certainly explain this Order's significance for the Roman Catholic authorities. However, the Order, it is said, began to fade here after the death of Charles II, but was revived in Sweden under the patronage of their monarch, Charles XII. (Some comments on the claim of pre-18th century origins will be attempted and left with the text at Mark Masons Hall.)

What is particularly worth noting is that Bolt's Grand Chapter faded out after his death in 1793, although his Lodge continued and became No.5 on the roll of the Grand East of the Netherlands. What is important for us to record is that since that time neither his rite, nor the Order of David and Jonathan as we know it, have been worked in Holland. What has just been recorded, therefore, calls into question the idea that the true origins of our Order were in the Netherlands. Not only was the practice there more complex, and certainly of a more strictly Christian nature, but the shortness of the Bolt Chapter's existence and the discontinuance of anything like the Order of David and Jonathan in Holland after 1793, makes connection appear much less likely. That conclusion is reinforced when one reads the judgement of Brother Waite, which is that 'there is not least reason to suppose that it derives from the Dutch Roman Catholic Order of Jonathan and David which was instituted for the propagation of the Latin faith and could have been neither Masonic nor secret'. (Vol.II p.217)

We therefore need to turn to another trail and one that has evidence of real continuity. We know that from at least 1765 there was an Early Grand Encampment in Ireland, and under its auspices many appendant degrees, which must have been in existence previously, were arranged as a series and authorised. It was through the influence of this body that not only were its appendant degrees and Orders warranted by separate agreements for use in Scotland but by 1790 the Early Grand Scottish Rite had been established and at first worked forty-one degrees, from the 4th to the 44th. In that series, the 12th to 16th were worked in a Royal Ark Mariner Lodge and the 16th was known as the 'Order of Brotherly Love'.

It would seem that this was the source of the degree that bore exactly the same name and number in an American set of less frequently used or extinct ceremonies known later as 'The Grand College of Rites'. No.16 in that collection, the 'Order of Brotherly Love', had as its jewel an ancient bow that was crossed with three arrows. As is stated earlier in the series, this degree was conferred in an Ark Lodge which was raised for that purpose. (That raising is on p.10 of the Grand College of Rites collection). In order to show, in comparison with our present practice, how similar or otherwise this is, I here give the Grand College wording.

[The Master, Noah, rises and gavels once. S. and J. rise and are addressed thus]

N: Sons S. and J., what are we thus met together to celebrate in the 16th degree?

S: That though the lad knew not anything—

J: —David and Jonathan knew the matter.

N: And why was it thus?

S: Because he loved him…

J: …As he loved his own soul.

N. Is there any Brother of inferior degree present to be taught a lesson by such love as this?

J: A. B., a Brother tried, and proved, is anxious to benefit by the teaching of Brotherly Love.

N: You will cause him to be admitted, and after listening to the teaching of the holy writings, let him be conducted to the E. for O. B. and instruction.

[N. gavels and S. and J. sit.]

J: Brother Guide, you will introduce Brother A. B. in regular form.

[The Guide conducts Candidate into Lodge, and halts him before J. and says:]

G: Brother J., I present to you Brother A. B., a Brother tried and proved for instruction.

J: Brother, you will listen to a lesson from the sacred writings [reads I Samuel, chapter 20]. You will now proceed to the E. for further instruction.

G: Father N., I here present to you A. B. a Brother tried and proved who, having listened to a lesson from the sacred writings, wishes for further instruction.

N: Brother A. B., before I can give you further instruction in this degree, you must take a pledge of secrecy. Are you willing to do so?

Candidate: I am.

N: Then repeat after me:

'I, A. B., on my sacred honour as a man and as a Mason, do pledge myself to keep secret from all persons not entitled thereto, the secrets of this degree, and confer it on no one without the authority of the E. G. [Early Grand], nor speak upon the same unless he be a Brother of this degree, and then only if he has come by it as lawfully as I have; and that, if I see a Brother of this degree doing anything detrimental to himself, or to Masonry, I will warn him as taught in this degree; and if ever corrected in like manner, I will pause and study before proceeding further. If I fail in this, may I be pierced to the heart with an arrow.'

N: Brother A. B., the secrets of this degree consist of a sign given thus [in each case the item is explained]; a grip thus; a C. W., answered by ( ); a P. W. and words of caution which we use thus:

Should you see a Brother of this degree about to do anything which would be injurious to himself or to the Order, and you have no other means of giving him warning, either from the presence of other persons not of our Order or otherwise, you will say ( ); if, on the other hand, you see a Brother hesitate in doing that which he ought, in like circumstances, you will say to him ( ), when he should pause and reconsider his action. Brethren, this degree, called the Order of Brotherly Love, is calculated in an eminent degree to inculcate those principles which, though dwelt upon in all the degrees of our Masonic systems, are here taught in a particularly striking form by the example which we have in David and Jonathan: a love which continued through all their chequered lives until death claimed one, and the other tells us that he 'loved him as he loved his own soul'. And what love could be greater? May the lesson thus taught be impressed upon our minds, and may we apply them to our Brethren on our road through life.

[End of this ritual.]

Present members of the Order of the Secret Monitor will be able to make their own assessment of how this extract from a series of American degrees at the start of the 19th century compares with what they are accustomed to today. They will notice that whilst the story of David and Jonathan is read, the title of the degree is different and there is not a link between that and the degree secrets that occur later. Above all it is evident that there are no opening and closing ceremonies, and no Rituals Nos.2 and 3. The fact that at that stage the degree was conducted within an Ark Mariner Lodge certainly explains why there was no need for some of the now accepted, additional portions.

What is important for our present study is that what we have here is a form of Freemasonry that clearly seems to have been practised in the USA by brethren who were, or had been, familiar with a similar Early Grand Encampment and its constituent parts in the British Isles in the latter 18th century. The oft-repeated suggestion that this appendant degree was brought to America by Jewish immigrants seems unlikely, if only in terms of the time-scale. The Dutch charter for practising this set of degrees was applied for only in 1788 which is after the Jewish brethren were introducing degrees on the East Coast of the USA. It is, I believe, far more likely that the originators were members of military lodges that had Irish or Scottish Lodge warrants permitting them to practise these Encampment extras. Was the Order of Jonathan, David and Jesus Christ just such a typically expanded, continental knightly version of what had been known in Scotland before 1780?

There could, however, be a connection between some of the elements of the Amsterdam Order and Orders elsewhere. I mention 'elements' only, because all the American evidence we have points to a one-degree ceremony and not a triple one. The comments of the 1964 historian of the Order here are worth noting: 'These [Dutch degrees] were very simple and had more the atmosphere of a secret society than a friendly brotherhood'. He goes on: 'It is possible, however, that Dutch migrants, working from memory, introduced fragments of it into the USA, working on the principle that any Lodge could work any degree provided it had a brother who knew the ritual.' Yet the fact that even in the Netherlands the Chapter that worked this degree had come to an end in 1793 and no copies of the book used by Brother Bolt were made or circulated certainly would have required memorising to be the method of any communication of it. This would definitely have had to be so with the Jewish Masons in the Rhode Island lodge in 1785 because they were introducing a series of degrees, and not just one.

In the light of this uncertain chain of events it does begin to seem much clearer that the basis for our own Order of the Silent Monitor is by the military acquaintance with the workings of Early Grand Encampments. As this is something that subsequent events may help us to decide, let us look at the next stage of the story.

Where a form of Secret Monitor degree appears historically, as in the 1831 'Ritual of Masonry' exposure produced by Avery Allyn, it is normally as one of a series of varied degrees. In the case of this latter production there was an affidavit signed by Jarvis F. Hanks who testified that the Secret Monitor was one of the several degrees that he had received. The Secret Monitor was also one of the degrees controlled by the Sovereign College of Allied Masonic and Christian Degrees for America. This fact was to have significant repercussions much later, but that is not part of this study.

For the record we might just take a brief look at the 'Secret Monitor', or 'Trading Degree' included by Avery Allyn in his 'Ritual of Freemasonry' of 1831.

This form of the degree is the first to state that it can be conferred by any of its members on another Master Mason in a lodge, private room or even out of doors provided that no cowan can discover them and that there is a Bible for the oath to be taken on. This then is the source of the reference to this practice by Keith Jackson at the outset of this chapter.

After exactly the same obligation to caution a Brother Secret Monitor about his behaviour as we met earlier there is now a rather more disturbing undertaking: 'I will assist a brother secret monitor, in preference to any other person, by introducing him to business, by sending him custom, or in any other manner in which I can throw a penny in his way.' There is a similar connection with business dealing when the signs, or actual words, are given since by the raising or lowering of a finger or by certain phrases there can be the advice as to whether to proceed or desist 'in any traffic or dealing to his profit and interest'.

It is because of the commercial and alerting aspects of this form of the degree that it ceased being called the Order of the Brotherhood of David and Jonathan and had a new title, 'The Secret Monitor or Trading Degree'. Considering the preferred principles of our own Masonic behaviour, particularly as regards avoiding brotherly favouritism, it was a title to be thought about afresh as it came to these shores.

The next significant stage of our story concerns a Dr. Issachar Zacharie, an Englishman who, though trained as an orthopaedic specialist, served as a surgeon in the American Civil War. Following that conflict he settled in California and took a prominent part in Masonic affairs there. In 1875 he returned to England, established a medical practice in Brook Street, Mayfair, and continued his Masonic interests. Having been advanced in the prestigious Bon Accord Mark Lodge in 1882 he met a number of brethren who had acquired the degree of the Secret Monitor elsewhere, one in Malta in 1845, one in the West Indies in 1846, and another in Jerusalem in 1848, all being places with strong British military connections. Brother Matier, an eminent Mark Grand Secretary, had received the secrets from an American brother in London in 1865. It is notable that all the recipients of the degree spoke of the ceremony and signs as being very simple which reflects what we have recorded in the US examples. After consulting with these brethren Dr. Zacharie called a meeting at his house for May 1887. It was as a result of this meeting that the first Conclave of the Order was founded and named the 'Alfred Meadows No.1', though in due time it became Premier Conclave, Number One.

By July 1887, a Grand Council of the Order had been formed with Dr. Zacharie as the first Grand Supreme Ruler. It was at this point that we can appreciate the further comment that though the Grand Council of 1887 first accepted the American style of ritual, that was rediscovered eventually inside the front cover of the First Minute Book, the principal founders apparently thought that a 'trading degree' was unworthy of the Order they were now reintroducing to these shores. Three members were charged with making any necessary changes whilst retaining the simple core of the ceremony as almost identical with the version given earlier.

It was thus that the distinctive characteristic of the Order as we know it was inaugurated and stressed as vital. It was, of course, the appointment of *not more than* 4 Visiting Deacons, whose duties were generally to assist and have a care for the other members of the Conclave, especially those not able to be present. The question, of course, arises as to how this feature was conceived since it is agreed that both the English and American versions owe their origins to a common source. What is quite clear from the US rituals is that members of this Order were meant to be aware of and be actively concerned about the behaviour and welfare of their brethren. That was the whole ethos of an Order of Brotherly Love and why the story of David and Jonathan was so apt an example. In the 1964 History Brother Wilkinson comments as follows:

'…it would be interesting to know whether the Visiting Deacon idea was rejected by the Americans, or was it an innovation sponsored by Zacharie, Spratling [the first Grand Recorder] and Philbrick [a Q.C. and the first Grand Chancellor]? It is clear from the early minutes that Spratling was largely responsible for drafting our rituals, in collaboration with Zacharie and Philbrick, and that [these rituals] were published in the names and under the copyright of those three.'

Since there is no mention of specific officers being charged with this caring function in any earlier extant form of Monitor ritual, and no reference in the 1887 Constitutions to any such tradition being either honoured or restored, it would seem most likely that it was a practice begun by the Order's first English leaders. They might, as a doctor, a lawyer and a Bachelor of Science, have correctly surmised that if the laudable aims of this kindly degree were to be more than simply pious phrases then some practical arrangement of this kind would not only help to achieve its longstanding aims but mark out the Order as distinctive.

If, however, this degree was now isolated from its previous links with other degrees and Orders, such as that of the Ark Mariner, matters of necessity, such as opening or closing a Conclave and installing a Ruler, had to be addressed. By October 1887 we have notice of a revised ritual being approved, and in the following year there were the draft rituals of the Second and Third Degrees to be accepted and ordered to be printed. Whether the 2nd degree ritual owed its origin to the 3rd Amsterdam degree emphasis on Princes is a matter that needs more reflection. It is obviously a real possibility because it was Spratling, we may recall, who first mentions that Dutch rite in his brief 1907 survey of the Order. That text must therefore have been available for them to consult. By 1889 the Rules and Constitutions for Provinces and Districts were issued and the approved clothing was worn for the first time. The Order much as we know it had arrived.

The Hidden Origins of the Cryptic Degrees

Surely the least researched of all the so-called appendant degrees, perhaps unsurprisingly, are the Cryptic degrees. In order to begin that search for more information we have at least one very useful pointer given to us by Keith Jackson:
'The Grand Council of Royal and Select Masters of England and Wales ... was formally constituted on 29 July 1873 by 4 Councils chartered just two years earlier by the Grand Council of New York' (p.24).

This makes at least two matters clear. The first is that at some earlier point the steps that we take, as a unified progression towards attaining all the degrees of this Order, were not originally so connected. That is a matter that we shall in part usefully pursue without having to look across the Atlantic. Secondly, however, it is clearly the case that if we are to understand every stage of the history of these degrees before 1873 we will have to include some study of the development of North American Freemasonry in the early 19th century.

In order to start an investigation of the degrees in their British setting it is worth looking at a few more words by Keith Jackson in his section on this topic. He writes:

The degrees in this group are frequently referred to as 'Cryptic Degrees' but such a description is not strictly correct as only two actually refer to a crypt. It is somewhat surprising to note that for many these ceremonies constitute nothing more than interesting side degrees or a random collection of unrelated incidents in the story of KST [King Solomon's Temple], but to the serious and understanding Masonic student they prove to be the essential link between the degrees of Master Mason and Royal Arch Mason. (p.24)

These are well chosen words and certainly represent the journey that I have made as one who has spent nearly 50 years in the Order. At first they seemed to be intriguing dramatic playlets that perhaps fitted somewhere in the larger Masonic pattern, but it was only many years later, as I properly began to appreciate the 18th century 'lectures' and their presentation of the Temple theme, that I saw how and why the sequence retained in these Royal and Select Master degrees was of such particular value. I must, of course, agree with Brother Jackson when he adds, 'the strict chronological order of events [in the degrees] is this: the S[elect] M[aster], R[oyal] M[aster], M[ost] E[xcellent] M[aster] and S[uper-]E[xcellent] M[aster]'. That order, in my view, is something that might with great benefit be pointed out to all members of this Order from time to time so that they are relieved of any sense of confusion as to what this group of Masonic experiences is all about and where they fit into the whole range of English Freemasonry. Other parts of what follows in this chapter might also be of interest and help.

What clearly happened in the latter part of the 18th century was that additional information began to be provided for what were usually called the 'lectures', which were among the main ingredients of a Masonic meeting. It is important for us be clear about this. The normal practice in lodges in the 18th century was for the candidate to be led round a table in the centre of the lodge room, to pass behind the Wardens and through the 'gates' which they symbolically represented and guarded, and then conducted over the floor tracing to make an obligation in front of the Worshipful Master. The candidate would then be invested with an apron and/or collar, and seated at the centre table while the Master either began to ask questions of the members in turn in the form of a catechetical lecture, or, with the help of the Past Masters, delivered a set of narratives such as the ones we are familiar with in the third degree historical account. What is now more apparent is that as an increasing number of Jews joined the Craft so a still richer content of traditional and legendary knowledge was provided for in these narratives.

It was this part of the proceedings which was curtailed, or else wholly omitted, after the Union of the Grand Lodges in 1813 even though the promoters of the Sussex or Emulation form of ritual eventually produced a separate set of lectures that, sadly, were less and less used and are even unfamiliar to many Freemasons today. It was in the pre-Union lectures, though, that many historical, or supposedly historical, events were recorded that were accordingly in danger of being wholly lost when the use of such lectures was dropped or reduced in content after 1813. It was this information, in the minds and memories of some brethren, that led them to ensure that such material should not be lost and is why not a few bought the lectures that were on sale from Brothers Finch and Carlile during the period 1790-1830. Those provided by Finch included the degrees of Past Master, Excellent Mason and Super-Excellent, whilst those presented by Carlile had Secret Master, Intimate Secretary and Excellent Mason. A mention in this latter title of

'Mason' rather than 'Master' need not disturb us because those degrees could only be taken after a brother had been through the Chair.

In addition to these instances we ought to note that in the West of England there were several degrees worked. In 1777, a John Knight was installed as a Knight Templar, probably in his Royal Arch Chapter (sic) at Devonport, after which he was admitted to the last seven degrees of the twenty-six (sic) which made up Masonry there. In 1811, he wrote in a notebook about this Rite that was practised in some lodges from about 1770. We find that amongst others were No.9: Excellent or 81 Deputy Grand Masters; No.10: Super Excellent or Nine Supreme Deputy Grand Masters.

Brigadier Jackson, writing further on this matter in his invaluable book *Rose Croix*, tells us that the:

Excellent and Super Excellent degrees were being worked in England from c. 1730 [sic] but died out quickly, possibly from lack of support, active antagonism or their suppression by the Royal Arch degree .... As we do not know the rituals of the originals, it is impossible to say whether John Knight's degrees were revivals of the early English group or new degrees from France. All the degrees in this group [7-18] have to do with the completion of the Temple or its rebuilding after the Babylonian captivity … All the degrees have a similarity with degrees of the Ancient and Accepted Rite. (p.130)

These texts were surreptitiously preserved and copied in some areas of England during the time when it was generally considered incorrect to use them openly, i.e. before the Duke of Sussex died in 1843. After that date these and many other degrees and Orders made their reappearance, e.g. the Knightly Orders, the Rose Croix and the Mark.

There is, of course, the other side to the story so far as the progress of the so-called Cryptic degrees is concerned. During the latter half of the 18th century French Masons had multiplied the number of degrees available and in 1756 there was a Council of Emperors of the East and West which worked twenty-five degrees known as the Rite of Perfection. Just for the record it was the conflict between this body and the by then established Grand Lodge of France which finally resulted in the forming of a separate body there that is still called The Grand Orient.

It was in 1761 that the Council of the Emperors issued a patent to a Jewish brother, Stephen Morin, to spread the Rite of Perfection on the American continent. Authorised to create Inspectors in those places where the Sublime Degrees were not practised, his work flourished. The records in North America indicate that the first Lodge of Perfection was established in Albany, New York State, in 1768 and bodies of the 'Sublime Degrees' were established in New York city by the 1790s. The degrees of Royal and Select Master were thus brought to those shores by Inspectors General of this Rite of Perfection and were worked as 'courtesy degrees' in the States as early as 1783. In May 1801, there was another important step when the Supreme Council 33° for the United States of America was begun at Charlestown, South Carolina. In view of what was said above it is worth our noting that there were four Jewish members of that Supreme Council. What is also noticeable is that prior to this date only twenty-five degrees were recognised, although thirty-three degrees had been known in the Primitive Scottish Rite begun at Namur, France, in 1770. Many of those degrees, however, were different from *any* in the list of this new American Council. What this latter fact clarifies is that whilst we may note variations of title amongst the degrees mentioned, we know that the names refer, partly or in full, to similar forms of ritual. We will have to return to this matter before we finish.

Carrying our story forward it can be briefly stated that control of the Secret and Royal Master degrees by the Supreme Council of the Ancient and Accepted Scottish Rite was relinquished when separate Grand Councils of Royal and Select Masters were established in various places. In Canada, for example, the degrees seem to have appeared for the first time in 1820. John Barney, a Masonic lecturer from Charlotte in Vermont, USA, visited several lodges in the Eastern townships of Lower Canada. He was invited and paid to speak about Craft work but also to organise Chapters of the Holy Royal Arch, the Mark and other degrees including the Royal Master and Select Master. He not only conferred these degrees on brethren but helped them to form Councils for each which would ensure their proper continuance and extension. That he was successful is proved by the fact that in 1821, 1823 and 1824 there are extant records showing that Councils were regularly conferring these parts of what is now our Cryptic Rite.

The other factor that we have to consider is the input of the military lodges in which additional steps were encouraged and performed, and it was in the developing areas of the British Empire, especially in North America, that the military lodges registered their greatest influence. It should be no surprise that material for the separate parts of what we call the Cryptic degrees should have been maintained and promoted by members of the newly formed District Grand Lodges of the Eastern seaboard of both the independent United States and provinces of Canada. It was in these areas that the military lodges would have been active prior to the US Declaration of Independence. The legacy they left in the United States was to persist even after they had withdrawn and it was a legacy in two senses.

As the vast majority of the military lodges were warranted by the Irish or Atholl Grand Lodges it was the practice for these bodies to be allowed to work more than the three basic degrees under a Lodge warrant. The presence on the American continent of a clearly richer mix of ceremonies was just what had once impressed Thomas Dunckerley as a naval Master Gunner and convinced him that the premier Grand Lodge back home must provide an opportunity for its members to be more than merely three degree Masons. He was by no means alone in recognising the appeal which the additional degrees exercised for many in the Fraternity.

A similar development is seen in 1826 when Samuel Kidder, another lecturer from the USA, was forming Royal Arch Chapters and Cryptic Councils in New Brunswick, and by 1828 meetings of the Council of Royal and Select Masters in St. John, the capital, were advertised in the city newspaper. Though this in fact proved to be a somewhat short-lived, home-produced presence we next learn that in 1866 the Council of Select Masters in Baltimore, Maryland, USA, conferred this degree on Robert Marshall of St. John with the purpose of establishing the rite again in New Brunswick. A year later Marshall was authorised by the Grand Council of Maine to establish three Councils of Royal and Select Masters, and following their creation a Grand Council was formed locally. What this is telling us is that active United States Councils in the early 19th century were able and willing to extend the usage of these two Cryptic degrees. We should hardly be surprised to learn, therefore, as we did at the start of this paper that a Grand Council in New York, which had formed four degree Councils, eventually gave authority for the forming of a Grand Council for England and Wales in 1873.

The first conclusion we can draw from all of this is that what is preserved in these degrees has a much longer history than we might have imagined. It was from Britain that these degrees took their rise at least a century prior to the forming of the Grand Council of 1873, and the Super Excellent degree had roots in English practice that take it back to another half-century before then. Just because the present authority may seem to owe its immediate existence to

American influence does not mean that such are its only roots. Rather, what this tells us is that even if mainstream English Masonry was severely trimmed back after the 1813 Union there were enough representatives of the older ways in overseas parts to preserve what could so easily have been completely lost at home.

A second conclusion has to be that what tended to conceal both the existence and the significance of these four degrees is first their emergence here as elements in separate Orders of Masonry and their continuance in the States in what became two other collections of degrees. What is meant by this is that whilst the Select and Royal Master degrees were promoted as parts of the Ancient and Accepted Rite of Perfection, the Super-Excellent Master degree belonged originally to a Royal Arch sequence of the 1810 early Grand Scottish Rite and the Most Excellent Master was a preliminary step in a Knight Templar setting, nowadays part also of the additional degrees of the Order of Holy Royal Arch Knight Templar Priests.

The creation in the United States of two major Masonic 'pathways' – the York Rite and the Ancient and Accepted Rite – which can be taken by Master Masons there, meant that these four degrees each needed to be ruled separately and that is why, as we saw above, there were four Councils brought together by the New York Grand Council.

It is the combination of these degrees from different backgrounds that probably helps to explain why they are now taken in a illogical sequence.

But were the Cryptic degrees in continuous use?

In 1810, John Fowler, one of the most distinguished of all Irish Freemasons, made a list of the ceremonies then being practised in that land. His list included the following: Past Master, Excellent Master, Super-Excellent Master, Arch and the Royal Arch. Of these degrees the Excellent Master was, though not identical with our Select Master, at least sufficiently similar to allow for a continuity to be seen. The Super-Excellent degree was clearly the precursor of what is called the ceremony of the Veils today, but in so far as it was then held in what was called the Court of Babylon it was obviously related to the setting and purpose of the degree of that name in our present sequence. Both led up to the circumstances of the Jews being freed from exile. The 'Arch' degree was simply the earlier name for the Most Excellent Master degree.

The lectures by Finch, albeit not ceremonies, included the same content as the Excellent and Super-Excellent above, whilst Carlile's Secret Master contained much, and more, of the Royal Master. His Intimate Secretary relates in part to the Select Master, whilst the Excellent Mason has elements of our Super-Excellent. It can thus be seen that whilst there are persisting threads, there were continual refinements before the degrees as we know them finally returned to this country.

The final conclusion, then, has to be that gratified as we may be that we have these interesting steps available for English Freemasons, there is a sense in which unless, as with the Mark degrees, we are clear about how they were originally intended to enlighten the path of a Mason toward his ultimate goal, we can be left with a sense of their being pleasant but sideline steps in the whole Masonic scheme. When the 'Select Master' degree is connected with those Craft words regarding Hiram's final burial place, 'as near to the Holy of Holies as Israelitish custom would permit', or a secret only shared when all three Grand Masters were together; when the Royal Master degree is shown to be connected with the items Hiram made 'in the clay grounds of Succoth and Zaredatha' and also the devotions that occupied him at noon each day; when the Most Excellent Master degree is seen to be the completion of the Mark Master degree and the essential introduction to the Arch; and when the Super-Excellent degree is seen as the historical preliminary to the full exile story assumed in the Holy Royal Arch; when all these parts are put in context is it any wonder that among our forebears there were those who were determined to preserve and restore these portions of the whole Masonic panorama? Surely there cannot be any doubt that we have to do all we can to explain both their antiquity and their purpose.

Where Did the Various Allied Degrees Come From?

In *Beyond the Craft*, Keith Jackson tells his readers that it was only in 1879 that a 'Grand Council of the Allied Masonic Degrees was formed, to bring under its direction all lodges of various Orders who recognised no central authority and were not regulated by the other major governing bodies'. Four of the present Allied Degrees were then included, but we are reminded that some 18 years later the Grand Council took the Grand Tilers of Solomon, one degree of the Secret Monitor and the Order of Holy Wisdom or Holy Royal Arch Knight Templar Priest grades into its care; only the first of these was retained to form the current range of five Allied Degrees.

It was in February 1870 that there appeared, in *The Freemason* magazine, a letter written by a Masonic historian of growing repute, W.J. Hughan, which suggested that it was perhaps time for the formation of an all-embracing Council of Rites that might reduce the number of governing bodies for several additional degrees. Whilst there is no evidence so far that this useful suggestion was immediately acted upon, it is true that in 1873 certain degrees were incorporated into what was called the Grand Council of Royal and Select Masters, whilst in the same year the Grand Lodge of St. Lawrence Masons, which had been essentially a Northern activity, secured a London branch and would thereafter include other Southern venues.

The official history of the Allied Degrees tells us that it was in 1875 that the next mention of a proposed corporate body to regulate the many other individual rites was made by a Brother K.R.H. Mackenzie to his uncle, the Grand Secretary of the United Grand Lodge. While there appears to have been no response to this further suggestion, the idea was now being at least considered by Masons of some influence. The result was a letter inviting any interested parties to meet at Alexandra Palace on 9 August 1879, ostensibly to carry out an Installation of the Master in the Metropolitan Lodge of the Order of St. Lawrence but also to transact 'other business'. That business included a proposition that there should be a Council of Side Degrees which those involved in other degrees were invited to join. The new Grand Master of the Mark Degree, Canon Portal, was elected as the first President, and the Grand Secretary of the Mark, Brother Binckes, agreed to act as the first Secretary. By 1 January 1880, the name of the new body had been changed to the present title of Grand Council of the Allied Masonic Degrees. The progress, and practice, of the degrees with which we Allied Degrees members are familiar was now assured.

What must now occupy our attention is the answer to the question, where did these additional degrees, that were now to be more suitably administered, come from? Did they have homes to which they originally belonged and if so what were they?

If, as is often stated, they were mere 'side degrees' then to what were they related, or did they have a totally separate existence and purpose? It is to the solving of those queries by delving into their past that we must now turn.

Searching for an Early English Masonic Sideline

In 2002, I was invited to deliver a talk at a lodge in Todmorden, Prudence, No.219. As luck would have it, my investigations benefited significantly from this invitation.

I discovered that in Todmorden, situated right on the Lancashire and Yorkshire border, before the establishment of the present oldest lodges there, there had been a Lodge of St. Lawrence which not only had distinctive features in its ritual and practice but also reproduced some of those on its form of summons. The Wardens pictured there stand at the foot of the two great Pillars and are not only dressed in plain white aprons but stand one with his left arm akimbo and the other with his right arm likewise. Such a stance was called 'elbow square'. This representation might, in other circumstances, have been thought to be simply a quirk of an artist's or engraver's imagination, but on a summons relating to a lodge named St. Lawrence the clear connection with their ceremonial practice was too close to be a mere coincidence. It showed that here was something unique in English Freemasonry from the 18th century which had been kept intact by this earlier Calderdale Valley Lodge.

Nor was that all. When the Prudence Lodge eventually replaced that of St. Lawrence as the regular Craft Lodge in Todmorden it not only took over the style of its summons, but has preserved up to the present day a very distinctive practice during the course of the Installation of a new Worshipful Master. The Past Masters of the Prudence Lodge are informed that this unusual practice was adopted here because it came to them from the earlier lodge of St. Lawrence. Here was another direct link with the local past.

Following this visit to Todmorden it happened that I began to look at some older copies of the Manchester Lodge of Masonic Research Transactions. In Vol.XXXI/1941 a talk by a Major Jeffery is included on 'The Additional Degrees of Freemasonry'. In this paper we find the following passage:

> Knight of St. Lawrence the Martyr. This originated at Colne, Lancashire, about 200 years ago, and appears to have been started by operative masons to distinguish themselves from 'these newfangled speculative Masons'. (p.20f)

A search through the records of Colne Masonry has yet to completely confirm Major Jeffery's claims, though there are traces of early Masonry in Colne which show that at exactly the period when the St. Lawrence degree was said to have been introduced there was a 'Freemasons or Friendly Society Holden at the Hole in the Wall in Colne'. This is supported by the report, in the Minutes of the Royal Lancashire Lodge No.116, that also met at an inn called the Hole in the Wall, of the death of a Brother John Shackleton in 1782 and the report at that point that he had been a member of 'that Lodge for upwards of 50 years'. As the Royal Lancashire Lodge was warranted only in 1760 this entry cannot mean that he was initiated into Royal Lancashire but that he was a Freemason in the earlier Society though now celebrating his fifty-plus Masonic years in this regular lodge. The date of his initiation must have been about 1730, and as there is no indication that he was a founder of the earlier Society, the start of that body must have been sooner. When you consider that the date claimed by Major Jeffery for the St. Lawrence degree was some 200 years back from 1939 you can see how the dates fit. What we now know at least is that there were Colne Freemasons of an older vintage than those of the premier Grand Lodge and when it would still be natural for many working stonemasons to be in the membership.

At this point, of course, it occurs to me that there may be some brethren present to whom the mention of St. Lawrence in a Masonic context is quite unfamiliar. For their sake I shall at this point introduce some further evidence. In a book originally written by a Brother Harold Prestige entitled *The Allied Masonic Degrees* (first published in 1979 and revised by Brother Frederick Smyth in 1999) we read as follows:

> 'No reason has been found to doubt the validity of the claim, accepted by Hughan, [a noted early 20th century Masonic historian] that this degree [of St. Lawrence, the first of the constituent Allied Degrees] dates from at

the latest 1750. It has the prima facie appearance of being based on a medieval mystery [play] that was designed to commemorate the martyrdom of the saint in Rome on 10 August 258 and adapted, probably in Lancashire [and Yorkshire] to distinguish genuine operative masons from the speculatives who were joining Craft lodges in increasing numbers.'

The book also makes a further reference to a date about 1735 when the ritual of this degree in Lancashire and Yorkshire was in much the same form as it was in 1885: 'Even today the ceremony ends by congratulating the candidate on his admission "to perhaps the only relic left to us of operative masonry".' (p.67) I personally would query that last statement, but let us leave that for possible comment later.

What is interesting is that there are features of the earlier forms of this degree ceremony which are no longer practised. The degree was once conducted in a Lodge formed as a Craft Lodge and with the knocks of such a Lodge, for it was not then the case that a member of this Order had to be a Mark Master Mason as is now the requirement. The prayers used were addressed to 'the Grand Master of all' and the Bible, on which the candidates were required to take their obligation, was opened at St. John's Gospel, chapter 1, as we know was a usual practice in the 18th century, for Antients Lodges at least. Differently, however, from today's St. Lawrence practice, the Bible was then laid on top of a miniature gridiron that was initially hidden. It was only in the subsequent 'lecture' or catechism that this implement, the symbolic as well as the actual tool of the saint who was reported to have suffered martyrdom by being grilled thereon, was displayed and commented on.

It is also worth noting that this Order possessed at its outset its own Installation ceremony and it is this which was eventually chosen as the necessary Installation form for the ruler of a whole Allied Council. This is most interesting because the content of this Installation ceremony is clearly operative in style and bears no relation whatever to any of the other degrees conferred in the Allied series. On the other hand, a link to this Installation form with that of the one in some Northern Craft Lodges has already been indicated. What is even more revealing is that until this degree was incorporated in the Allied Degrees sequence the title for a ruler of the St. Lawrence degree was 'Right Worshipful Master', another connection with 18th century English Craft custom and not simply in, or from, Scotland.

As proof of the retention of this older practice the Prestige/Smyth book quotes from a notice in *The Freemason* magazine of 25 January 1879 which reads as follows:

> The installation of this [a St. Lawrence] lodge was held at York on Wednesday the 8th instant. Brother George Simpson, Senior Warden and Right Worshipful Master Elect was presented and questioned, and a Board of Installed Masters having been opened [Note: not *declared* open] he was duly enthroned in the chair.

It is also noted that when the Installing Master was putting the questions to the Master-elect he particularly demanded that he should be given 'unequivocal replies'. Moreover, there is one early Allied Council which still requires the Master-elect to be presented by two Past Masters, a custom not unknown in some older Northern Craft Lodges.

The book by Prestige/Smyth tells us one more thing that is relevant to our search for origins:

> In 1870 the Masonic authorities in England that remained independent of the Craft and the Royal Arch [included] the Grand Lodge of St. Lawrence Masons at Rochdale, Lancashire, with a number of subordinate lodges ... There were also some unconnected bodies in various parts of the country, but mainly in Lancashire, working without any control, various unrelated grades of NO direct interest to any then existing authority. (p.9)

Following the Union of 1813, when other than the three Craft degrees were not encouraged, the St. Lawrence degree must have continued to operate because of evidence given by another Brother Shackleton, who is alive today and in his nineties. He has put on record that Mark Masonry was being practised in Todmorden in 1848, some 14 years before the consecration of the present Temperance Mark Lodge of which he is still a member. He further states, 'It is more than likely that the founders of the later Temperance Mark Lodge were brethren of this Lodge of St. Lawrence Masons because the brethren who are stated as W.M., S.W. and J.W. on the [Temperance] warrant ... figure prominently in the Minutes of the Lodge of St. Lawrence Masons.' (Information from a privately owned lecture.) I have now tracked down those St. Lawrence Minutes, but have not succeeded so far in seeing them. At least we know that they existed within living memory. Whether the creation of Temperance Mark Lodge led to the closure of the St. Lawrence Lodge, or whether the latter then moved to Rochdale, as we noted from the Prestige book earlier, is also not known. We are at least a lot clearer about the practice of the St. Lawrence degree in this area for more than a century. More research must obviously continue.

Returning, however, to Colne as the suggested centre for the start of this Masonic practice, five questions still need answering. The first is why was it necessary to have a further degree that would distinguish between the operative and Accepted Masons? For an answer we need to look at the overall development of the Masonic Craft in England.

What happened in certain cities and towns of England from the 15th to 17th centuries was that trade guilds had been formed; amongst these there is evidence that, where there were sufficient stonemasons locally who were eligible as Freemen, a Masons' Company or Guild was part of this system. The distinguishing feature of such a Guild was that in addition to the Guild Court there was attached a lodge in recognition of the earlier lodge system that prevailed on working sites. As we know from at least Chester, York and London, these Guild Lodges began to admit Freemen of other trades who, though not members of the stonemason's Craft and hence not normally eligible for sharing in the Guild Court and its trade business, were 'accepted' into the Masons' Lodge. Why this was so and why other than stonemasons should wish to share in the traditions and customs of a Masons' Lodge has been explained by me in *York Mysteries Revealed* and would be too long to repeat here. Suffice it to say that it happened, with the result that by the 1670s in York and the 1680s in Chester we note a move by some stonemasons to apply for a new charter to establish a fresh guild or company which would represent only those who were actively engaged in their trade or other closely allied ones. Such charters were granted, but what is revealing is that there were some stonemasons who still continued to belong to the older Guild body which, though it had now lost its 'trade' function as a court of craftsmen, still existed simply as a Lodge. Indeed, it seems clear that such Lodges regarded it as essential for there to be at least some working stonemasons for them to continue to claim to be a body of Freemasons. Their presence would ensure that certain customs and forms would be authentically preserved.

That led, however, to another twist in the development that was now taking place. As the Lodge section was no longer linked to a trade guild there was no certainty that those who joined the Lodge had ever been apprentices as had once necessarily been the case with all those who attained their local Freedom as craftsmen of any trade. There thus began to be a three-way division of candidates: those who were bona fide working stonemasons who were Freemen, those who had been apprenticed in other trades and became Freemen, and those who had *never* been apprentices in any trade and so were not Free of any craft. It can be well imagined that this led to some hard decisions that had to be made in a Lodge. Who was really fit to be accepted as a Mason and what was now to happen about Apprenticeship? Certainly those who were already qualified craftsmen stonemasons would object to being readmitted as Apprentices, but how were such men to be identified?

It is just at this point that a degree such as that of St. Lawrence begins to be introduced and to make sense – it distinguishes the operatives from the others, and yet it can satisfy the operative members by excusing them from any preliminary degrees. One can see why it would have been devised. The second question is why was it called St. Lawrence and apparently started in Northern areas? The answer lies in the involvement of the trade guilds in the town plays of the late Middle Ages. We know that in Lincoln 'there were alternatives to the otherwise annual Mystery plays, i.e. Saints plays which portray the conquest by their namesake of some particular vice. [on 10 August] I am fascinated to find St. Laurence who conquered Avarice by his display of Charity.' (Op. cit. p.8)

One drama historian suggests that it is from this evidence at Lincoln that we can begin to see how the Pater Noster (Lord's Prayer) plays were created, viz. by having each of the 7 petitions of that prayer acted out as separate playlets, each on a different cart or moving stage called 'pageaunts', and with a different saint featuring in each play. We know that such a processional performance took place in York in 1389, and we also know that when such a type of play was performed in Beverley it was the masons who presented the one in which Avarice was overcome by Charity. The story of St. Lawrence, a church deacon, was that he was cruelly put to death because he would not disclose the secret of where the riches of the church were, those riches in fact being the poor folk whom he and others cared for; and when we see that he was martyred by being tied to a gridiron made up only of squares and right angles it is hardly surprising that such a story would appeal not only to the medieval Christian workmen but also have a lasting symbolic significance. To those familiar with even our present Craft ritual the connection is clear.

We come then to the third question: in what way would such a degree be incorporated into the accepted Masonic Craft system? When a Lodge was manifestly no longer part of a Craft Guild system, where established rules of membership obligation applied there would be occasions on which a working stonemason might apply to become a member of an Accepted Lodge. He might rightly claim that he had no need to undergo the usual step of Apprentice, having been through that process in his mason trade. To permit such an exception to the rules some kind of test would naturally be required and not least by any of the same trade who were already Lodge members. It is therefore likely that this St. Lawrence form of ceremony would be held during a special day or time when the applicants for this privilege might be examined by their trade peers. Whether the degree was permitted to be seen by other members who were not stonemasons we do not know, but is it not a singular relic of common usage that whenever Masons are asked to give their consent to a proposal made in open Lodge they use the sign that originated in this degree – the arm held square to the body and extended forwards forming a right angle. That at least is how the consent sign began and its source as the sign used by stonemasons may well be because it was that act which operative masons informed others was the traditional method or by seeing it used by them.

But when and how did this Order cease to be part of the normal Masonic system? Probably first in the decline of stonemasons as members of Accepted lodges and especially after the rise of the working trade unions, which bodies borrowed, as we know, from Masonic ceremonies and usages. There can be no doubt also that following the Union of 1813 this and many other 'additions' to Craft Lodge workings, as with the Mark degrees, were disapproved of and widely discouraged. Only in some areas were such practices treasured as 'traditional' and preserved for occasional use. That is why in such culturally and religiously conservative areas as Yorkshire and Lancashire we find this degree and others persisting to the latter 19th century and the forming of bodies ruled from Mark Masons Hall.

Some evidence does exist that this degree was practised in other parts of the country, though when the invitation to discuss the Order's future was issued to interested bodies in 1879 by the Metropolitan Lodge the only southern body traced with certainty was the Escurial Lodge, Havant, near Portsmouth. The name Escurial, of course, was singularly fitting because one of the most prestigious and ingenious of palaces built for Philip II in the late 16th century was the Escorial near Madrid. It was built on a gridiron pattern and was dedicated to, and consecrated on the feast day of, St. Lawrence.

For the record, the other Masonic bodies extant in 1879 were the Escurial Lodge of Sheffield, Ebor of York, Paragon of Hull, an unnamed lodge at Bottoms and those in and around Rochdale. There is not, however, any current mention of a body at Colne. It is for this reason that the degree has always been considered a Northern usage and for the reasons already amply given it certainly carries that sort of cachet. If Wigan was the banner bearer of older Craft tradition in the post-Union era in one regard those who held on to the St. Lawrence degree were of the same stock. At least we can now begin to give them a somewhat more pronounced profile.

Finding the Knights of Constantinople

Of all the Masonic practices featured in this book this would appear to be the one of which the purpose and certainly the sure origin are still elusive. In the official Introduction to the Ritual of this degree, it is constantly repeated that this is a real 'side' degree, in the sense that, many years ago, it was customary for one brother to confer it on another (by taking) him aside at the end of a lodge meeting, administering a simple obligation and entrusting him with the secrets. Yet this apparently clear and straightforward explanation still raises several queries.

What sort of time-scale are we talking about when there is the phrase 'many years ago'? Since we know that this degree was being worked in America in 1831 we are talking about at least 175 years. However, this cannot be the full extent of the degree's existence if we take into account the further statement in this ritual's Introduction: 'from the strong flavour of Operative influence in the ritual it may be conjectured that it arose during the transition from Operative to Speculative Masonry'. If that is the case, and I would concur with that view, and not least when we see the form of the degree which still prevails in Plymouth Working, then we are proposing a much earlier date for its introduction 'as a side degree'.

With such an earlier period in mind as a possibility it is much more reasonable to consider afresh the suggestion made in the Freddie Smyth (Allied) lecture by Right Worshipful Brother Brian Price when he writes:

> 'Its origin, although circumstantial, is interesting with a possible connection to another local Craft Lodge. Amphibious Lodge was warranted in 1786 at the Marine Barracks, Stonehouse, near Plymouth, where in the 19th century there existed the Ancient and Honourable Order of the Knights of Constantinople. Amphibious Lodge came to the Calder Valley in 1802 and may well have brought the degree from Stonehouse. This differs somewhat from official history so additional research is needed.' (Op. cit. p.10)

Since the official view is that military lodges were the disseminators of this degree to America in 1831 and to Devonport in 1865, it hardly seems outrageous to suggest that it was by means of another military, or naval, lodge that the degree could have been introduced at the outset to Amphibious Lodge even as early as 1786.

Another obvious question is what was the lodge working that must have prompted someone to feel that this avowedly 'side' degree was needed? The most natural answer here is that it was one of the newfangled knightly degrees that started to come in from Ireland or the Continent through the extended workings permitted under a Craft warrant held by a military or naval lodge. If this is so, then we are talking about any time after 1760 and though this was long after the period of transition from operative to Accepted that was mentioned earlier, it was, as I know from my researches in York and Chester, still a time when operative stonemasons who were members of an Accepted Lodge could, and did, complain about the manner in which it was thought that Freemasonry was being altered for the worse.

The scenario suggested is that an Antients Lodge, or one warranted by the Antients, introduces a new Red Cross working that begins to claim that only those who are worthy enough can now aspire to this new eminence in the Craft. By the time this new practice has begun to be more normal it would hardly be a surprise if one or more of the operative members were not to take a freshly installed knight, especially one who was to be a 'Knight' of the Red Cross of Constantine, and try to give him a salutary lesson in humility and modesty. It was no more and no less an abiding tenet of English Masonry to 'acknowledge that all men are equal in the sight of the Most High'. This was operative masonry once more seeking to preserve some influence on its Accepted offspring.

The likelihood of this being somewhat closer to the origin of this degree than has been thought hitherto is provided by the background history of, and the presence of various features in, the Plymouth working of the Knight of Constantinople. Even though this working does not start in Devon until 1865, it appears to have come via a military connection with Gibraltar and Malta. What strikes us is that in the period 1814 to 1825 'Waller Rodwell Wright, the Chief Justice in Malta, drafted a grandiose scheme for a 'Red Cross system' to include several then existing Orders' (Allied history p.71). These facts serve to confirm that there was not only a Red Cross knightly context to this degree but that the idea of a military or naval communication of it was likely.

To all this we have to add these 'marks' of this working which certainly confirm for me that this was something from the mid-18th century rather than the 19th. First of all it is specifically Christian. The Sovereign asks the candidate: 'Are you a Christian?' and the reply includes the words, 'I am… and profess myself a devoted follower of the lowly Nazarene'. When introduced into the universalist atmosphere of a Masonic post-Union England and, according to the record, 'believing it to be the only Council in England possessing the degree, styled it the St. Aubyn Grand Council…' confirms that they are here establishing what they were sure was the original nature of the working. And what is the response of those who are then asked to confirm the admission of a new Knight? 'O yes, O yes, O yes', and the Chief of the Artizans reads out the natural proclamation that follows that 18th century call: 'You are known as good men and true…'. The same true meaning of the repeated 'O yes' is confirmed when a Brother says at the end, 'O yes, O yes, O yes, We proclaim Sir Knight…. as a Knight Companion of our Order…'

In an even more pointed fashion the Plymouth working stresses the knightly connection with a Marshal, Heralds, a Seneschal and a Prelate, presentation of a sword, a bannerette and a six-pointed star of Bethlehem. It is also significant that the use of an implement, which denotes the penalty of the degree, is a symbol that, though preserved in the 3rd degree of the Scots Master Mason, was dropped in England after 1813. The various lectures in this form of the degree also revive certain notions of pre-Union practice and certainly overlap significantly with the Red Cross of Constantine Order, thus again suggesting that it was first after the introduction of that knightly aspect of Masonry that a side-degree was timely, certainly for old-time masons.

Discovering the Grand Tilers of Solomon, or Masons Elect of Twenty-seven
We cannot yet be sure about the origin of this degree. Indeed, when we learn that it not only has two names but has also had several others denoting ceremonies that tell a very similar story, we need hardly be surprised. Keith Jackson is the one who suggests a trail of puzzling discovery by telling us, 'Under an early title of SELECT MASTERS of Twenty-seven, this degree is known to date back in America to 1893'. He then tells us that it relates a 'story of the accidental intrusion of a craftsman into the secret vault of KS [King Solomon] where his fate is determined by the three GM [Grand Masters]'.

This is a legend remarkably similar in purpose to that of the Cryptic degree of a Select Master (p31), but also to the 6th degree of the Ancient and Accepted Rite called 'Intimate Secretary'. We also have a degree entitled 'Intimate Secretary, obtained by Curiosity, or English Masters' in a Manual of Freemasonry that was compiled and published by Richard Carlile in the 1820s. So why are there so many different titles for what was meant to be almost the same event in our Masonic experience?

What forms the core of this particular Masonic experience is a consultation by the Grand Masters in a location that was taken to be so totally secret or private that there was no need to provide a doorkeeper. However, the conversation is overheard by a mason who discovers the entrance to this meeting place to be partly open. He is then discovered as an eavesdropper and his fate is decided by the Grand Masters because he now possesses secrets beyond his station.

It is as we appreciate the circumstances of this tale that we begin to understand the reasons for the varied titles given to the degree. The description of Masons Elect of Twenty-seven derives from the idea that:

…the place where the Grand Masters met was in a subterranean vault under the Temple that had been constructed by 24 Fellowcrafts or Menatschim. One of the brethren of that grade being the eavesdropper it was then decided to limit the number of those to be admitted into this degree should be at the most 24 who, with the 3 Grand Masters, become 'Masons Elect of Twenty-seven'. By reason of the fact that the person who became privy to the secrets was either an 'intimate secretary' of Solomon called Joabert, a favourite of that king called Manon, or a master craftsman called Zabud, we can begin to unravel the descriptions of the participant who obtains secrets by curiosity or becomes a Select Master.

We also learn that in the Oriental Order of Mizraim the eighth grade is called English Master and hence the alternate names in the Ancient and Accepted Rite are a Perfect Master by Curiosity and Perfect English Master. The rank bestowed on those who have penetrated thus far into the palace apartments, or to the vault under the site of the Temple, is appropriately that of 'Grand Tiler', lest anyone else unauthorised should seek to penetrate places forbidden and so that a holder of this title may learn the lesson of keeping secrets inviolate. We learn from the accepted history of the Allied Degrees that there was a degree known as the 'Select Masons of Twenty-seven' in the United States in 1761, and from what we know of the degree's description it would certainly seem that this is a form of what we call Grand Tiler or Intimate Secretary. By then the Ecossais degrees, including those that had begun to expand the exploits involving Hiram and those who followed him, were becoming well established in France and the United States. As is described in the chapter on the Ancient and Accepted Rite there was a real, if doubtfully authorised, Morin's Rite of 25 degrees in 1762, and certainly the 'Perfect Master by Curiosity and Intimate Secretary that some lodges also call English Master' are steps that are firmly included.

This latter mention leads us to the fact that in 1746 there was in a once operative lodge of stonemasons meeting on Tyneside at Swalwell a notice that read as follows:

MEMORANDUM OF THE HIGHRODIAMS

Enacted at a Grand Lodge held that evening that no Brother Mason should be admitted into the dignity of a Highrodiam under less than ye charge of 2.6d, or as the 'Domaskin' or 'Forin' as John Thompson from Gateside pd. at the same night 5/-.

N.B. The English Masters to pay for entering into the sd. Mastership 2.6d pro majority.

In the light of one of the alternate titles given to the degree English Master, one wonders if such a degree was already in existence in 1746. Certainly we know that the Ecossais degrees, of which this was one, were already being produced on the Continent from about 1740 and so there is no doubt about its being available by this time. What is also interesting is that in a book of 1756 that gives details of the brethren that were 'Raised to the Herodim' is a mention of the 'Passed the Bridge' degree being taken. This is, of course, another name for the next degree in the Allied series, the Red Cross of Babylon, thus showing the existence in this North-eastern area of another Ecossais grade. What is more, this mention suggests that there was obviously some way of conveying these new Masonic stages to Britain.

With regards to what has just been said it is clearly a possibility that, as the Allied Degrees history says, 'There was an 'Order of English Masters' at Swalwell in 1746'. On the other hand there could be an alternative way of interpreting the Memorandum shown above. We cannot here enter at any length into the still intriguing study of what exactly was Harodim/Heredom practice in the North-east of England, but its outline was a course of several lengthy catechetical 'lectures' which were delivered by teams of Past Masters, revealing the past 'history' of Freemasonry and its symbolic characters and events. There can be no doubt now that it resembled the same 'Heredom of Kilwinning' practice that was taking place in the London area at exactly the same period. As also happened in the south of England, the Harodim practice began to fade once the Mark, Arch, Royal Arch and Knightly degrees began to emerge as separate degree occasions.

Bearing this type of Masonic practice in mind we can see that no Freemason was allowed to partake of the Harodim unless he had paid the fee of 2/6d, a not inconsiderable sum in those days. As I suggested in my book, *The Arch and the Rainbow* (p.53), a higher sum of 5/- was charged to the brother from Gateshead for a further stage of the Harodim, the Templar or Domaskin/Damascene rite that had been imported or was now known as 'Forin'. If this latter explanation is right then it once again confirms that there was a knightly element to this *Beyond the Craft* instruction just as there was in the London Heredom practice.

What this means for our purposes, however, is that when the Memorandum states especially (and hence NB – *nota bene*) that English Masters are also to pay 2/6d to enter the said Mastership it could mean not that this is an early mention of the Order of Grand Tilers or Masters Elect of Twenty-seven, but something else. It has to be recognised that though the Swalwell Lodge had sworn its allegiance to the premier Grand Lodge in 1735, it remained essentially an operative lodge until 1779, a fact that reveals itself by calling itself a 'Grand Lodge' in this Memorandum. What can thus be inferred is that it regarded the Past Masters of any lodges acknowledging the London Grand Lodge as 'English Masters'. What could be meant by this footnote is that if qualified visitors from other English lodges would be welcome, they would still have to pay the normal fee for admission to the 'Harodim lectures'.

Whilst we cannot wholly rule out the presence of this as a very early appearance of the degree that we have been tracing, this latter suggestion as to what the term 'English Masters' might mean does allow for the truth of the Allied history's statement: 'there is at present no certainty that the degree of Grand Tilers … had been worked in England before Matier obtained it from the USA in 1893' (p.75). What we can be sure of is that it would have been in existence under one of its names by the middle of the 18th century and been practised by French and military lodges on the North American continent.

The Route of the Red Cross of Babylon

'This degree,' says Brother Jackson, 'is of considerable antiquity being closely associated with the Holy Royal Arch and the rebuilding of the second Temple of Jerusalem with the candidate bearing the name of Zerubbabel.' As with the preceding degree, the long existence of the Red Cross of Babylon is witnessed to by its variety of descriptions since it first appeared. The names come from the various Rites from which all or part of the present practices derive. The compilers of those Rites included a series of degrees and 'in each series the scene is set partly in Babylon and partly in Jerusalem but, wherever the series begins or ends, there is, in the middle, a short but important episode of crossing a bridge over a river'. The river in question was either the Euphrates or the Jordan.

It should, therefore, occasion no surprise that the earliest known name is 'Passing the Bridge', and soon afterwards we note the 'Babylonish Pass'. We next have 'Masonry renew'd or the Sword Rectified' and fifty years later 'The Red Cross Sword of Babylon'. In the Ancient and Accepted Rite it has the immense title of 'Knight of the East, of the Sword, of the Eagle and Knight of the Sword of the Red Cross', while when the Supreme Grand Royal Arch Council assumed control of this and other degrees in the early 19th century this was called 'The Red Cross of Daniel, Jordan Pass and Royal Order or Prussian (or was it originally Persian?) Blue'.

The terms 'Bridge, Pass, Jordan' now all become meaningful and when we learn that the party returning from exile under Zerubbabel was provided with arms and training in their use, the word 'Sword' becomes relevant. The term East refers to the direction from which the Jews took their journey back to Jerusalem, and the 'Eagle' reminds us of God's promise to those other exiles returning from Egypt: 'I will bear you up on Eagle's wings and bring you to myself.' The latter reference to the prophet Daniel was a reminder of a faithful Jew, despite his exile in Babylon, and the mention of Prussian Blue should in reality be the Royal colour of the Persians, as of all Middle Eastern monarchs. The real colour was Tyrian purple. The tradition of the Prussian king, Frederick, being associated with the Ancient and Accepted Rite accounts for what looks like some confusion here.

Whatever the variety of titles, however, there is a steady line of practice for this Red Cross degree. It is worked in the Baldwyn Rite of Bristol under the title of the 'Knights of the East, Sword and Eagle' before the Knight Templar step and with this Encampment we are at once looking back to 1780 at least. At about the same period there are rituals of the old Mark Man degree in which the 'bridge motif' is part of that story which tells how a Mark Man needs to return to Jerusalem to be able to complete his task as a Mark Master. His journey is impeded by those who would prevent him crossing a river on his way. It is then in the period 1764 to 1790 that De Lintot's Rite of Seven Degrees had a fifth degree that had two parts covering the return of the Jews from Babylon and the rebuilding of the Temple, and this had also been taken by Morin for his 1762 Rite. Nor is this all.

We have a mention of this degree as 'Passing the Bridge' in 1756 and we also know that in nearby Sunderland the Antients lodge there was working the same degree in 1755. It is no surprise, therefore, when an earlier author of the Rose Croix history, Brigadier Jackson, tells us that 'the Rite of Harodim, practised in the North-east till the Union, had (some) degrees which were basically the same' as those of the Ancient and Accepted Rite. He further states: 'The degree of the Knight of the East appeared about 1750 to allow those, upon whom it was conferred, to control the Perfection and Elu degrees.' As an extension of one of the seven or eight degrees formed for use in a lodge in Bordeaux in the years around 1750 we can claim this as the actual origin of the Red Cross of Babylon.

The Sacred Roots of the Grand High Priest

A.E. Waite said about the Grand High Priest in his New Encyclopaedia:

> The priesthoods are many in Masonry, from those who are ordained [sic] to the Office of Joshua, son of Jozedech, to those who in less frequented ways may still be Priests of the Sun, though it must be confessed that the rank has suffered a certain substitution. (1921 Edition, p.295)

Considering that the range of priestly elements which Waite implies does mention the Holy Royal Arch Knight Templar Priests (see p93) but not the Degree of the Priestly Order of Israel, or Provost and Judge in Carlile's Manual, we might at first be a little confused as to where the Order of the Grand High Priest, that is our main concern, fits.

In the Freddie Smyth lecture for 2005, Right Worshipful Brother Brian W. Price tells us that:

> In the early 1800s, in Manchester, The Mother Tabernacle of High Priesthood was working a version of Grand High Priest. By 1815 three Lancashire Union Bands had been warranted … [and] From 1819 to 1871 minutes and accounts record Priestly Order meetings at Bottoms, with over 100 brethren consecrated into the Order. (p.9)

What has to be clarified here, however, is whether it was still the Grand High Priest or the Holy Royal Arch Knight Templar Priest ceremony that was being constantly practised. The new history of the latter Order tells us two things. First is a reminder that:

> a Schedule of the degrees worked by Royal Kent Tabernacle [in Newcastle on Tyne] ... included 'Grand High Priest' ... to which was later added, by the Grand Secretary of the Allied Degrees, 'or the Templars NE PLUS ULTRA'. To confuse matters further, in the Agreement that was subsequently negotiated between the Knights Grand Cross [i.e. the Templars] and the AMD [Allied Masonic Degrees], the latter is stated to have under its authority the Order of Grand High Priest. This Order was formerly restricted to the [First] Principals of the Royal Arch but this qualification was lifted in 1934. (*The Priestly Order*, p.40)

A second mention in *The Priestly Order* is connected with the work of Harold Voorhis entitled *The Knights Templar Priests* (1968). This knowledgeable Mason mentions that:

> ...[in the 1829] archives of the Supreme Council 33° of the Ancient and Accepted Scottish Rite of the Northern Jurisdiction [there is on] the inside of what is otherwise a catechism of another Order a notice of the Priestly Order, but no details are given ... [Voorhis affirms that] a comparison of the extant rituals of the two Orders shows that they overlap, and that the Priestly Order comes first. In an American Royal Arch Chapter the Installed or, in some States, elected High Priest, representing Joshua in the English Order, is qualified to seek membership of a State Convention of the Order of High Priesthood or of Anointed Priesthood. The degree of Grand High Priest is worked in England as one of the Allied Masonic Degrees. (Op. cit. p.154)

Sadly, there is no clear indication as to what the overlapping Orders were or how they so overlapped, though this quote at least supports the suggestion that a Grand High Priest degree existed in 1829, that it had a particular relationship with the Royal Arch and, in that Order, was linked with Joshua, who, in the USA, was the First Principal of the Chapter. These facts confirm what was the case in the original Constitutions of the 19th century Grand Council: admission to this degree was possible only for those who were installed Principals. Even though that restricted access was removed in 1934, it explains why ordinary Holy Royal Arch members of the Order are still referred to as 'Excellent Companions'.

Staying in America for the moment we are informed in the historical introduction to the present Order's ritual that an Order of Melchizedek (this name being that of the somewhat mysterious kingly character who literally distinguishes the degree) had been accepted from Europe and was being practised after 1780 by Royal Arch Chapters in Massachusetts, USA. In 1789, we are told a 'William Rean was anointed after the Order of Melchizedek to qualify him to preside, according to the customs of St. Andrew's Chapter, Boston, at the time of election as Royal Arch Master of the Royal Arch Lodge [sic]'. By 1799, the General Grand Chapter had approved the ritual, and then in Webb's 'Masonic Monitor' of 1802 it appears as the 'Order of High Priesthood'.

What we next know is that as far as the European origin of this degree is concerned there were two possible sources. One of these was what was called either 'Order of the Asiatic Brethren' or 'Knights and Brethren of St. John the Evangelist in Europe'. The Order was started in 1779 by J.H. von Eckhofen, who was a private counsellor to the King of Poland. The Order had its centre in Vienna and was composed of five grades originally, two of 'novices' and 'seekers' and three superior grades of 'Knights and Brethren initiated from Asia in Europe' , 'Royal Priests or true Brethren Rose Croix' and a 'Melchizedek or principal' grade. A sixth grade of this Order had the same name as the fifth, 'Melchizedek or Royal Priest', but was one of the ceremonies carried out after 1780 and designed for the Jewish Masons who were ineligible for admission to St. John Lodges, which were strictly Christian.

Considering the close relation of the Grand High Priest Order with the Holy Royal Arch, it is of interest to note that those who were the 'ultimate superiors' in the Asiatic Order were known as the 'Fathers and Brethren of the 7 lesser known churches of Asia' and their meeting was called the 'Minor but Perpetual Sanhedrim of Europe' which was composed of 72 members. All that is further known about this Order is that it revealed strong cabalistic influence and appears to have faded in Austria by 1787. Brother Voorhis has discovered traces of its working by former members in France and other continental places, though these all disappear by 1800.

There may have been two sources for the beginnings of this Order and certainly there is the suggestion that the presence of two distinct themes in the present ceremony (the blessing of Abraham and the consecration of Aaron the Levite as the first Jewish High Priest) suggests that there may have been an amalgamation of two distinct degrees. Whereas the appearance of Abraham can be accounted for in the Melchizedek Order, it could be that the consecration theme 'was added at a later date to provide a High Priest of a Royal Arch Chapter, or to enhance the dignity of the First Principal' (*Introduction to Ritual* p.4).

That introduction stresses, however, that 'present evidence is that the principal elements of the ceremony are not derived from the legends and traditions of 17th century English Masonry, but are descended from one of the alleged 1100 "High Grades" invented on the Continent in the middle of the 18th century'. Brother Voorhis does suggest that there could have been a link with a rite called the 'Brothers of the Golden & Rosy Cross', which was itself a revival of a 17th century Rosicrucian fraternity which was organised in 1710 by a priest called Samuel Richter in Saxony. For the present that seems to be as far back as we can take the origins of this Order. What is certain is that the ceremony is very old and was worked in 'Antients' lodges, especially in Lancashire and Yorkshire. That certainly begins to suggest that the military lodges acquired the idea of the degree as the proper, mystical completion to the Holy Royal Arch. Its loss as the culmination of what we rightly regard as the *summum bonum* of English Freemasonry may be a cause for regret, but its retention as a significant part of the Allied Degrees ensures that it is still there to be appreciated.

The Ancient and Accepted Rite

Any attempt to uncover the origins of this distinctive 18th century form of Freemasonry, usually referred to in England as the Rose Croix, is now made even easier by recent publications relating to this Order. Essays by John Mandleberg, the author of the official history of the Supreme Council of the 33rd Degree for England and Wales, have most usefully complemented the previous account of Brigadier Jackson by explaining in more digestible stages, and for all Princes Rose Croix, how this remarkable adjunct to the Craft came to be and has successfully continued since. Where Keith Jackson tells us only that 'some of the degrees within this Rite may have had an earlier origin' we now have information that clearly enables us to consider the whole path leading to the Rite's first appearance in a fresh light.

In the first of the Rose Croix essays entitled 'The Birth of the Higher Degrees', the author writes:

> The publication of Samuel Prichard's MASONRY DISSECTED in 1730 marks a defining moment in the development of Speculative Freemasonry. We shall probably never know … how accurate an account it is of the actual working in English Lodges of three distinct Degrees, culminating in that of 'The Master' (see below). Its most important contribution is to put on to a firm narrative basis the Hiramic legend, the centrepiece from which almost every subsequent Order in Freemasonry is constructed and developed … The influence of MASONRY DISSECTED on the development of Craft ritual, both in the British Isles and overseas, can hardly be over-estimated. (Op. cit. p.13)

I recently discovered that distinctive features of this working are still in Lodge 29, founded in 1732. It has to be admitted, however, that this working poses a special conundrum. Whilst Prichard's Master Mason may be seen as a form of the accepted 3rd degree, it presents some features that indicate that it is 'The Master' degree in a different sense to what we regard as our own Master Mason.

For the benefit of any Mason for whom this may still be novel territory, let me point out that the password of this degree as related by Prichard is what is now the normal one in a Board of Installed Masters, the three candlesticks represent the Sun, the Moon and the Master who rules his lodge, the candidate representing Hiram Abiff is eventually interred in the Holy of Holies and on his coffin there is the name of God known as the Tetragrammaton. The fact that this Tetragrammaton still appears on the coffin in the Dutch third degree of Master Mason is one sure confirmation for me that Prichard is to be relied on as representing the practice with a third degree at that date. The question that remains is, was this the degree of a Master who was entitled to be the ruler of a lodge, either in fact or by virtue of this knowledge? Was this really a 'higher' degree because it elevated a man to the position of ruling over his Fellows?

It is on this whole matter of a desire for more eminent and hence 'higher' degrees, especially in France, that both our Rose Croix historians seek to shed more light. As Brigadier Jackson has said: '[In France] in its early days, masonry, unlike in England, was often an entirely upper class affair … patronised by the nobility'. Brother Mandleberg makes the same point: 'The aristocratic Freemasons had no wish to associate with such people [as wine-merchants and candle-makers] and looked for means of distancing themselves from them' and he continues: 'The evident response with which to resolve this dilemma was to invent new Degrees.' (p.14)

In France there then came what were called the 'Maitres Ecossais'. Both our authors are insistent that despite appearances these practices did not emerge from Scotland and, as with the similar but not identical degree of Scots Master in England, were only so designated to distinguish them from the now established 3rd degree. What is significant is that by 1743 there was first a Rule of the French Grand Lodge forbidding, and then two years later allowing, these Ecossais to have special privileges in lodges including special dress. The Ecossais even began to be known as Superintendents of Lodge work.

Two exposures of what was claimed to be the working of Ecossais Masons appear in 1744 and 1747 and then, just before 1750, there appeared a detailed ritual of a Rite of six degrees, with each of the last three relating in some way to what was to be the eventual list of what we know as the degrees of the Rose Croix.

What we have to recognise is that Freemasonry in France now entered a turbulent period. As Brother Mandleberg describes it:

It might be considered legitimate for sincere Freemasons to invent Degrees that filled the gaps in the Hiramic story, extending it to the completion of the First Temple, and even to the building of the Second … Towards the end of the 1740s it became 'Open Season' for the invention of 'Degrees'. The great majority of these had little relevance to what had gone before … it is not easy to navigate through this sea of ceremonies. (Essays p.22)

Fortunately there was a sea port where some kind of direction was being sought. That was Bordeaux and it was here that what began to be called Lodges of Perfection were principally promoted. In Bordeaux the Lodges tended to promote, beside the basic Craft degrees, those that continued to work degrees with more details of the Hiram story and also what were called the Zerubbabel degrees in which there was a continued search for the lost secrets. There were also Lodges of Perfection in Paris and certain other provincial areas and they seem to have been in the main those who propagated what were called the 'Vengeance', 'Elect' or 'Elu' degrees in which the discovery and punishment of the assassins of Hiram were portrayed. This variety of practice is but a small indication of the general turmoil which Masonry in France experienced up to the mid-1760s.

It was also during this period, however, that there eventually appears a 'Rite of Perfection' that is composed of 25 degrees. In this collection, all of which was of French devising after the 4th degree, we see the 18th degree, the one called Rose Croix, which only appears in a form approximating to the one with which we are now familiar by 1765. Its origin was mainly German, being associated with the 'Rite of Strict Observance', that was, in its turn, influenced by Rosicrucianism. By 1761, this degree – known otherwise by the titles Knight of the Eagle, of the Pelican, of St. Andrew or Mason of Heredom – was to have candidates who were known by 1765 as Sovereign Princes Rose Croix, a title with which we are still familiar today.

In addition, there now appeared the degree of 'Sublime Prince of the Royal Secret' which apparently originated in 1761 as the final degree of a series of 17 degrees. It was at once put at the head of the list as the 25th degree and this new number had come about after a disagreement in Paris over a body called the Council of Knights of the East. Most of these later degrees could at the time of their new listing have only been degrees by name, and it was probably not until 1771 that they had begun to have separate rituals. The 25th degree at that point was eventually to be the 32nd in the final form of the Rose Croix today.

There also stepped onto the Masonic scene a Stephen Morin. He was a merchant and French expatriate born to white parents probably in the island of Martinique. Admitted as a Parfait Elu Ecossais in the West Indies in 1744 he had, in between a number of visits to Bordeaux for both commercial and Masonic business, founded an Ecossais Lodge in Dominique, assumed the Masonic rank of 'Deputy Inspector', and finally, by joining a Parisian Lodge, obtained a petition that requested the Grand Council of the Lodges of France to give the right by Patent to promote Freemasonry worldwide. The Freemasonry to which this referred was, of course, of the Parfait Ecossais style.

On his return to the Caribbean in 1765 he first established a lodge called La Parfaite Harmonie which would meet wherever 'he may arrive or shall sojourn' and he then became Grand Master Inspector which gave him 'full and entire power to create Inspectors in all places where the sublime degrees shall not already be established'. He thus had control in such areas over the whole emerging system of Higher Degrees.

Morin, on a visit to Jamaica, now met Henry Andrew Francken who, though born a Dutchman, had now become a naturalised Englishman and an officer of the Vice-Admiralty Court. Being also a Freemason he was now granted by Morin, who surely must have known him, or of him, previously, the astonishingly high rank of 'Deputy Grand Inspector General of all the Superior Degrees of Free and Accepted Masons in the West Indies'. He and Morin were to work very closely together for the next eight years until Morin's death.

Their co-operation certainly produced results. They set up what is now generally referred to as Morin's Rite of 25 degrees and so as to regularise their work, Morin claimed that he had received the Grand Constitutions of 1762 from France. It is now generally accepted that it was Morin himself who compiled these regulations, probably in the years 1765 and 1766. Armed with both rules and rituals Francken took leave of absence from his Court duties, visited North America and set up a Lodge of Perfection in Albany and what is now the State of New York, providing it also with a warrant of authorisation.

When Francken returned to Jamaica it was to join in setting up the governing body of Morin's Rite. As specified by the so-called Constitutions it was called 'A Grand Chapter of Princes of the Royal Secret or Ne Plus Ultra' and Morin continued to promote its work until he died in November 1771 when Francken took on the mantle of leadership.

Francken continued to develop and clarify the various rituals of the 25 degree Rite and appointed several Deputy Inspectors General, one of whom was Major

Charles Shirreff, who, on his return to England, introduced other senior Freemasons to these additional degrees. We meet him in the story of the Red Cross degrees in this book. However, before the death of Francken in 1795, there was not a sufficiently strong guiding hand in controlling the practice of these additional degrees in both the West Indies and on the American mainland. The Inspectors, of whom there were about 80 by 1800, were somewhat lax in their selection of some of the 'new' degrees that were coming over from Europe.

The result was that the apparently established Rite of Perfection began to lose its former shape in many places and it was clear that a new controlling body was required. It came as the result of the efforts of two Frenchmen, the Marquis de Tilly, and his father-in-law, Jean Baptiste Delahogue. It was they who produced, in the words of Brother Jackson, 'out of chaos, something that has continued, unchanged in principle, for two centuries'. (*Rose Croix* p.62)

De Tilly was a French Army officer who was initiated in an Ecossais lodge in Paris. In 1789, he inherited his father's sugar-producing estates in Santo Domingo and went out to manage them, thus avoiding the implications of the revolution. He must have married in the island for his father-in-law, who was a local notary, then became a close associate in pursuing his Masonic activities. The first black rebellion took place in 1791, and de Tilly eventually became a regular officer in that conflict, but by 1795 the situation was so bad that de Tilly, Delahogue and their families moved to Charleston on the East Coast of America as refugees. They remained there until 1802 during which time de Tilly served as an engineer in the US Army.

Before they had left Santo Domingo both men claimed that they held the 32nd degree, though signing themselves as Deputy Inspectors General of the 'Francken' Rite of Perfection, that is, a rite of only 25 degrees. They continued their Masonry in Charleston, founding a Roman Catholic Lodge, and in 1801, de Tilly became Grand Marshal of the Grand Lodge of South Carolina. It was in the additional degrees of Perfection, however, that the two men sought to make their impact.

A Lodge of Perfection had been set up in Charleston in 1783 and a Council of Jerusalem, 16th degree, opened in 1788, but in 1797, the Deputy Inspector General in Jamaica, Hyman Long, gave patents to seven Frenchmen to set up a Consistory of the 25th degree or Princes of the Royal Secret. What the local Masons thought of this intrusion by 'foreign brethren' is not known, but Brother Jackson has shrewdly commented, 'It is conceivable ... that the known difficulties between the premier and Antient Grand Lodges [in England at this time] occupied all their attention'. (op. cit. p.65)

This was not the limit of de Tilly's ambitions. On the very day that he received his patent of the 25th degree from Long in Jamaica he issued a 33rd degree to his father-in-law. Unless he had received the appointment to do this during his short visit to Santo Domingo that year he was doing this on his own authority. Whatever the case, he was in 1797/8 signing, for others, patents as Sovereign Grand Commanders of the Supreme Council of the French West Indies, and Delahogue was on the Council as Lieutenant Grand Commander.

There is no record of what was happening until May 1801, but it is likely that, spurred into fresh action by the steps taken by their French neighbours, the locals were being helped to plan the start of an American Supreme Council. The French brethren were knowledgeable about the further degrees emerging from France and America and would benefit from the notarial skills of Delahogue in drafting documents. It was apparently not intended that the two Frenchmen should have any continuing place on the new Supreme Council, but what is unclear is whether de Tilly conferred the 33rd degree on the appropriate new Grand Commanders or those officers conferred it on themselves. The new Constitutions of 1786 allowed for the latter action to be possible because they clearly state that 'a Supreme Council of 9 brethren in each nation, who possess all the Masonic prerogatives in their own district that his Majesty (of Prussia) individually possessed … are Sovereigns of Masonry'.

On 31 May 1801, an impressive ceremony marked the start of the new Supreme Council of the Ancient and Accepted Scottish Rite. The inclusion of the words 'Ancient and Accepted' in their title suggests, writes Brother Jackson, that 'having been initiated into the Craft in lodges with a strong English background where the title was normal, [they] may not have wanted to widen the gap between the new and older types of Masonry'. (op. cit. p.68f)

The new Rite now had 33 degrees which set it in agreement with other European rites which also had that number. In the 1786 Constitutions there was a detailed explanation of how the degrees of the preceding 25 degree Rite were to be incorporated into the new Rite and which were the new degrees that were needed to complete the number. What is of interest is the fact that though the names and placing of the further degrees were decided, the rituals of some of them were not fully fixed for several years.

It only remains, for our purpose in this book, to look at what had been happening in England. The additional degrees that were practised in England in the period 1730 to 1750 began to disappear, and it was not until 1770 that any additional degrees begin to be revived or introduced, especially in the military. There were even individual Lodges at the turn of the century that worked a single Rose Croix degree. The more normal practice, however, was for the Rose Croix or Ne Plus Ultra degree to be worked as part of a Knight Templar Encampment as is still the case with the Baldwyn Encampment at Bristol. In those earlier days the Rose Croix could be conferred only on the Masons who had already taken the other Knightly Orders.

It is neither possible nor indeed essential to enter here into the details of the abortive offer of a patent to the Duke of Sussex in 1819 to form a Supreme Council. It is, however, necessary to record that by the time the Duke died in 1843 there were 25 Chapters, such as the Royal Kent in Newcastle upon Tyne and St. John of Jerusalem in Cornwall that were still working a Rosicrucian degree. It was this element of their workings that was to provide the basis for the final stage of our story as the Ancient and Accepted Rite emerged for England and Wales.

By reason of a patent granted to Dr. Robert Crucefix by the Supreme Council of the Northern Jurisdiction of the USA the first Supreme Council met on 1 December 1846, and by a process of downward bestowal members of the 33rd, 32nd, 31st and 30th degrees were duly created. There was then a meeting of the 18th degree, Rose Croix of Heredom, and the Order as we know it was launched.

Wherever Did the Red Cross Come From?

In seeking to answer the question posed by the title of this chapter I am tackling an issue that has constantly nagged at me ever since I joined this Order nearly 50 years ago. As with many of the dependent degrees, it is a topic that has hardly received a lot of attention and certainly not if you compare the amount that has been spoken and written about the Craft and the Holy Royal Arch. It is therefore not too difficult to find a point from which to begin and I start by looking, as I do so constantly in this book, at Brother Jackson's *Beyond the Craft*. What he so admirably provides as basic information may be brief, but it is generally correct. Let us then look at what he tells us about the 'Red Cross of Constantine'.

He says that the 'origin of this Order is surrounded by considerable mystery, for while mention is made of the Red Cross degree as early as 1813, it would be negligent to assume that the Red Cross of Constantine was the degree in question for there were a multiplicity of organisations around 1800 which had assumed the title of "Red Cross of…", all with rituals propounding widely different legends' (op. cit. p.42). Brother Jackson continues:

> It is worthy of note, however, that Robert Carlile, who was fairly accurate in his revelations, published an exposure in 1825 which featured a degree called the Red Cross of Rome and Constantine, and the working, while being a very shortened version of what is in use today, is still strikingly similar. It is therefore not unreasonable to assume that the Red Cross of Constantine was being actively promoted in the early 19th century and even possibly the late 1700s: but it is now an accepted fact that the establishment of the Order, as we now know it, was the work of Robert Wentworth Little who supposedly reconstituted the Grand Council with the assistance of W.H. White [the Grand Secretary of the United Grand Lodge] and W.J. Hughan [the later renowned Masonic historian] in 1865.

So much at least from Keith Jackson.

Now it also happens that in 1868 'Sir Knight' Robert Wentworth Little himself wrote a 'Sketch of the History and Records' of our Order so that we are able to discover what was his particular view of our origins. Limits on time and space mean that I am unable to reproduce the whole of this narrative, but here are the most salient points:

After the death of [the Emperor] Constantine the Order is said to have flourished but considerable obscurity envelops its history until the year 1190, when it was revived by the Emperor Isaac Angelus Comnenus. From this period down to 1699 the Grand Mastership was vested in the Comnenian family who were considered to be the lineal descendants of Constantine. The Grand Crosses of the Order continued, however, to exercise their undoubted privilege of conferring the Red Cross upon worthy men and we are, in all probability, indebted to the Abbé Giustiniani, who was attached to the London Venetian embassy, for the existence of the Order in England. It is beyond any dispute that the members of the English branch were, during the 18th century, men of high position in society and of eminence in the Masonic Order: though, as with the Knights Templar, we are unable to say positively when the order was restricted to Freemasons.

Brother Little goes on:

In 1788 under Major Charles Shirreff of Whitchurch, Salop [or Shropshire], several distinguished brethren of the 'mystic tie' were admitted [as Knights of Constantine] – James Heseltine, the Grand Treasurer; William H. White, the Grand Secretary; John Allen, Provincial Grand Master for Lancashire, and James Galloway, Past Junior Grand Warden.

He states further: 'About this period the Order of the Holy Sepulchre flourished, and in 1796 Lord Rancliffe, Grand Master of the Knights Templar, was also the head of the Red Cross and other chivalric orders.' This suggests that at this stage the Holy Sepulchre ceremony was attached to the Knights Templar Order. On referring to the Minutes of the Red Cross Order we find that the meetings were held at the Freemasons' Tavern in London, and Wentworth Little provides actual extracts from the Minutes to show the nature of the meetings held up to 1813.

These statements seem to offer detailed and convincing pieces of evidence pointing to the definite existence of this Order over 200 years ago, but in order that we might make a proper assessment of what Wentworth Little wrote there are three things that have to be grasped. The first is that whilst he provides an intriguing story of how the Order of the Red Cross of Constantine may have come to England, he is careful to indicate that at some point what was unquestionably a wholly Roman Catholic and ecclesiastical Knightly Order was either transposed into, or paralleled by, a Masonic Order with the same title and legend. It is known that a Catholic Red Cross Order continued into the 19th century and a Prince Rhodocanakis, when he was its head in 1878, made clear that there was no connection whatever between his and the contemporary Masonic Order.

That this was the case in 1878 is clear, but whether he also meant his declaration to be retrospective, that is, covering a duplicate organisation exactly a century before, we cannot tell. What would seem logical is that if, as Wentworth Little stated, Freemasons were made Knights of Constantine in 1788 then the Order which admitted them must have been a separate one. Indeed, some of the Freemasons mentioned as members at that time would certainly not have joined the Order if the Masonic branch had not severed its connections with a solely Roman Catholic body. That is especially the case if we recall that at this time Roman Catholics still had a restricted role in society. How such a 'duplication' of the Order came about, and when, Little does not suggest, though the inference is that it must have been before the 1788 meeting.

That inference suggested a possible subject for further research which has now been done. What transpires from further study is that as far as any English knightly Freemasonry is concerned, the Red Cross Order practised in London from circa 1790 does not appear to have been that of Constantine but of *Palestine*. The Minutes and ritual can be consulted in the library of the United Grand Lodge in London, and if this is the Red Cross Order which Little claimed to be restoring then he was either mistaken, misled or was himself misleading.

The next point that has to be stressed is that, as stated in the quote from *Beyond the Craft*, the ceremony connected with the Red Cross by the 1820s was a shorter version of what we are familiar with today. Robert Carlile describes the practice thus – the Grand Master is named Constantine and his deputy, Eusebius. There are two Generals, a Grand Standard-bearer and a Janitor. At the opening we are given the following dialogue:

Why do we open and close in this degree with 16 reports?

In allusion to the 16 stars surrounding the 16 letters comprising the Grand Words 'In hoc signo vinces' ...

How do we prepare our candidates for this degree?

In the clothing of a Roman soldier; the cross of Constantine in his right hand and in his left a New Testament.

For what reason?

To hold in commemoration the miracle that wrought the conversion of Constantine ... [and the whole story which we recount is then recited in full.]

Was there any other thing remarkable in the life of our royal founder?

The arms of his soldiers, the public prayer, his charity, and tomb. [These are all fully explained, and then follows a Catechism that shows in part the close connection with the earlier Roman Catholic Order.]

Why are we conducted round the Conclave 12 times when we are exalted?

In allusion to the 12 great pillars that support the Church of Rome. [The 12 points are then explained, especially in regard to Helena, the mother of Constantine, and her discovery of the true cross.]

[And it then closes with:]

What are the passwords?

Constantine and Matthias.

What is the chief furniture of this degree?

A grand transparent cross placed in the East formed by 16 stars and in the centre the letters forming the Grand Words.

What is the jewel and mark of this order?

A Cross with the initials of the Grand Words ...'

In the closing ceremony (and here using Carlile's own words) 'there is an invocation of 13 Saints, of the 12 Apostles and St. Paul, in the true Roman Catholic style'.

From where did Carlile obtain all this material if, as seems clear from what has been outlined earlier, this Order was not practised in English knightly circles? The answer is that he obtained it from a Scottish source, as he did much of the rest of his 'exposures'. That fact explains why many Masonic students in the past have been mistakenly led into imagining that some strange practices were occurring in English Masonry at this time.

Meanwhile it has to be observed that when Brother Waller Rodwell Wright became the Grand Master of the Red Cross of Palestine in 1804 he was also invested as the Grand Master of the Holy Sepulchre Orders. This confirms the view that there was obviously some connection between the two bodies, though there was not the progression from one to the other as is our custom today. What is also clear, however, is that from at least 1809 there is mention of the Noviciate of St. John the Evangelist as forming part of the Red Cross of Palestine Order. This is confirmed by the fact that when Brother Rodwell Wright went to Malta and instituted the Order of the Red Cross of Palestine he also practised the Noviciate of St. John as part of the whole ceremony. Where the Noviciate and Holy Sepulchre ceremonies came from is a subject that will be dealt with in the next chapter. What needs to be underlined is that some kind of link was being firmly established between a Red Cross ceremony, the Holy Sepulchre and a degree of St. John.

The third thing that has to be realised is that Wentworth Little was all too well aware that he had a political problem. By the 1860s, the forms of Freemasonry which had been agreed and promulgated at the 1813 Union of the Grand Lodges were very well established. That agreement had a significant clause: 'But this Article is not intended to prevent the Lodge or Chapter from holding a meeting of any of the Degrees of the Orders of Chivalry...' The only question then remaining was which were the legitimate 'Degrees of the Orders of Chivalry' then intended.

The Duke of Sussex had been associated with the Red Cross of Palestine, becoming Grand Master on 19 July 1813. If mention of Palestine was overlooked by later investigations, then when, in 1865, the Red Cross of Constantine appears as a regular Masonic activity it was declared to be 'revived', and not 'constituted' on the assumption it was the same as the earlier Palestine Order. There is, however, another possible route by which the Red Cross of Constantine degree could have emerged in the 1700s. To discover what this might be we need to examine a now very rare pamphlet written by a once very distinguished Scottish Masonic historian called George Draffen. The pamphlet is entitled 'The Red Cross in Scotland' and is part of our substantial Masonic library in York.

George Draffen was not only a senior Grand Officer in Scotland but a Past Master of the Quatuor Coronati Lodge of Research in London. He was also the most knowledgeable expert on knightly degrees in Scotland. On p.4 of this work he writes as follows:

The [Constantine] degree does not appear to be indigenous to Scotland; it was probably brought to this country, along with other 'High' degrees, sometime in the middle or latter part of the 18th century. As a conjecture it probably came from Ireland and could well have been brought over with the Knight Templar degrees. It was certainly part of the Early Grand Rite at the close of the 18th century … The Early Grand Encampment of Ireland was the first governing body over an 'omnium gatherum' [a general assortment] of Masonic degrees, unrecognized by either the Antients or Moderns Grand Lodges in England or the Grand Lodges of Ireland and Scotland. In Scotland [however] it was the practice of many Craft lodges to work any Masonic degree they fancied until in 1800 that custom was prohibited.

Brother Draffen then tells us that Scottish Masons journeyed to Ireland to receive such degrees, particularly in Cork. The Craft degrees probably remained as the 'key' ones, i.e. were always worked, whilst these others were performed only when a candidate especially requested them. The Early Grand Encampment of Ireland existed from about 1770, and though we do not know the full extent of the degrees that were authorised by that body we do know for sure that a Red Cross of Constantine was one of them. Yet if the Early Grand Encampment of Ireland is to have assembled and authorised the practice of all these degrees sometime around 1770 they must have been in existence *before* 1770.

What all this means is that in the 1760s some ceremony related to what we have today, even if much shorter, was being carried out in Ireland. The evidence that there was a Roman Catholic antecedent of this ceremony only adds to the likelihood of this being a source from which such a type of degree might naturally be derived. The fact of its being linked in Ireland with the other Red Cross degree of Daniel, of Andrew, of Patmos and of Palestine, and that these in their turn were connected with the Royal Arch and Knight Templar degrees, means that it was more than likely that they were known and practised in lodges that used all those ceremonies. This would be from at least 1759, which is the year when the earliest Certificate of an Irish Knightly Order is known to have been issued.

We thus have the Red Cross of Constantine degree appearing in an Irish setting in the middle of the 18th century, at just the time that many military Lodges were being formed, holding Irish warrants that allowed these additional degrees to be performed in a Craft setting. These military Lodges made their own special impression on British Masonry at home and abroad as the regiments to which they were attached served in worldwide locations. It is, for instance, more than likely that it was through acquaintance with such lodges that Thomas Dunckerley, the supporter and promoter of the appendant ceremonies, became familiar with Knight Templar Masonry and sought to establish it in England from the 1780s. I suspect that it was his influence and interest that led to the preservation also of the further degrees associated in the knightly family. This is either the genuine source of the Red Cross of Constantine that Wentworth Little wrote about or it was a strongly contributory factor.

A piece of evidence that eventually came to my notice supports the view just expressed. It indicates that Robert Gill (1756-1822) helped found the Cross of Christ Encampment of Knights Templar in 1795. This Encampment worked a number of degrees, and their records in 1796 show that they worked the Red Cross of Constantine. This is very important because what it means is that perhaps Wentworth Little was not referring to the Red Cross of Palestine after all. He must have known that Knight Templar bodies were promulgating the Constantine ceremony at the date he claimed. If he didn't know that then he was earning himself an unreliable name quite unnecessarily. He was in fact reviving a previous bona fide practice.

It can, therefore, I believe, be justly claimed that the Order to which we belong has been practised in some form and in some places for 225 years at least in England and probably for 250 years in other parts of our islands. Contrary to what might be otherwise inferred, this is not a late 19th century 'fabricated' Order. It is one that has a creditable pedigree of which we can be properly proud.

The Appendant Degrees of the Holy Sepulchre and of St. John Evangelist

The 'Historical Note' which precedes at least the 1973 ritual reads:

There is no connection, historically or ritually, between the Masonic Degree of Knight of the Holy Sepulchre and the medieval Military Order of the same name which is said to have been founded in the eleventh century.

The Military Order was associated with the Constantinian Order of St. George, sometimes referred to as the Red Cross of Constantine. The ceremony of Admission originally took place in the Church of the Holy Sepulchre in Jerusalem and details from the diary of a pilgrim who was received in the fifteenth century have been recorded by H.F.M. Prescott in her [book], 'Jerusalem Journey', London 1954.

There is much more in that note, but we will have to come to that later. There are three things that are intriguing and puzzling about this portion of the statement. The first is the fact that it was thought necessary to have such a statement at all, especially when one notices that in the 1917 edition of this working there is not the least trace of any such note. Why should that be?

The second intriguing matter is that whilst there is said to be no connection between the medieval and Masonic Orders bearing the same name, the earlier one used to have, and ours now has, a close link with the Red Cross of Constantine. Why should there be this apparent difference?

Thirdly, though it is apparently suggested as being of no consequence, we are given the details of where we can observe what took place in the medieval Order even though, we are here told, it has no ritual link with what we do today. All these matters do seem very strange. It is clear that we need to reflect on each of them a bit further.

Firstly, why is there such a note at all? Surely it must be because there were those in the last century who claimed that there was such a link between the medieval and Masonic ceremonies and hence the chiefs of this Order felt that they had to make plain that to hold such a view was either incorrect, undesirable or open to misinterpretation. Which reason, however, was the correct one? If the claim that there was a connection was incorrect then that surely has something worthwhile to imply about what is a strong current obsession with the theory that there was a definite link between medieval knighthood and its practices and our present Masonic working.

If the link was thought undesirable then that might well have something to do with the religious affiliation of the older institution. The Constantinian Order of St. George, which was both ruled over, and written about, by a certain George Rhodocanakis, was a wholly Roman Catholic one, and it was therefore very unlikely that any of our 19th century forebears would have wanted to be associated with that body. There was bound to be a refusal to allow the Masonic Order of the Holy Sepulchre to be linked with what was a totally Roman Catholic practice.

On the other hand it may be that this preliminary note reflects an attempt to avoid misinterpretation by addressing what is a real issue in this field of medieval and modern ceremonies. What I believe is the fundamental flaw in many of the books that claim knightly origins for Masonic practices (that is, books such as *The Hiram Key*, *The Templar Legacy*, *The Head of God* or *The Sword and the Grail*) is the contention that because there is some kind of similarity between what was done and said in those days with what is said and done now, that of itself proves a connection between the earlier and later bodies. Such thinking even led some of the early contributors to the Quatuor Coronati Lodge Transactions to make the mistake of wondering if recognisable Maori greeting signs proved their users to be primitive Freemasons. Perhaps this Note was inserted intentionally to combat such superficial thinking. If so, this too is to be commended.

Yet that cannot be the end of our queries. If there is a good basis for this Note it seems odd that an absence of connection between the Holy Sepulchre and the Red Cross or Constantinian Order should be stressed when a close association in several particulars is exactly what happens to represent the current situation.

When Richard Carlile produced his *Manual of Freemasonry* in the 1820s, he included a comprehensive degree called the Red Cross of Rome and Constantine. One feature of that degree is that in addition to much that we would recognise in our Red Cross ceremony of today there was the following Catechism which relates directly to both the Traditional Oration in our Holy Sepulchre degree as well as to the Installation part of our Red Cross series. Some of the wording of that section is as follows:

> What was the first Grand Point?
> The humility of Christ upon the Cross.
> The Second?
> St. Helena going from Rome to Jerusalem.
> The third?
> The pious and diligent enquiry of St. Helena after the sacred spot, Golgotha.
> The fourth?
> St. Helena finds three crosses, and is much perplexed to know which is that of Jesus Christ.
> The fifth?
> Macarius, Bishop of Jerusalem, directs St. Helena how to discover the cross of Christ from those of the two thieves.
> The sixth?
> The first public acts of St. Helena and Constantine after the cross of Christ has been found …

Apart from using the name Marcellinus instead of Macarius for the Jerusalem pontiff, these responses are a full summary of what we still use, and here it is still linked, as it was in the medieval form, with the Red Cross of Constantine. One still has to ask, then, what can the Note mean?

The mystery remains when we examine the reference made to the book by H.F.M. Prescott. The actual passages in question are on pages 138 to 140 and first of all describe an event during the pilgrimage around 1480.

> During the second visit [to the church] the noble laymen among the company were to be dubbed Knights of the Holy Sepulchre, and admitted to that order … The ceremony took place during the hour before midnight while the rest of the pilgrims roamed at will about the church…
>
> Of the ceremony itself, which took place in the innermost chamber of the tomb, we have three separate and conflicting accounts which … show, that for all the antiquity which is claimed for the order … there was no set ritual of conferment.
>
> De Caumont [a nobleman] had brought with him a Knight Hospitaller

from Rhodes to perform the ceremony. After Mass at midnight the Hospitaller gave de Caumont the accolade, 5 times in memory of the five wounds of Christ, and once in honour of St. George, and then, assisted by the still vested celebrant friar, delivered into the new knight's hand the naked sword, bidding him receive it 'in honour and reverence of God and of my Lord St. George'. De Caumont, having sheathed the sword, took an oath of 6 clauses: to guard Holy Church, to help in the recovery of the Holy Land, to defend his folk and keep justice, to keep his marriage holy, to do no treason, and to protect widows and orphans.

In 1483 a knight, Brother John of Prussia, facing the tomb, girded the most eminent of the pilgrims, the Count of Solms, with a sword and spurs. The Count was 'bidden to kneel, and to bow himself so that his breast and arms rested upon the top of the tomb. Thus kneeling he received, in the name of the Trinity, a threefold accolade. This done, Brother John raised up the Count, loosed the sword and spurs from him, kissed him, and respectfully said, "May it be for thy good."

Fifteen years later the same procedure took place in the innermost chamber of the sepulchre save that, after receiving the sword and spurs and kneeling down, the candidate partly withdrew his sword, laid two fingers of his right hand on the blade, swore to be God's knight and to keep obligations like those that were stated above. The same Brother John then drew his sword, struck the candidate on the shoulder, saying: 'Arise, knight, in honour of the Holy Sepulchre and the Knight St. George.'

When such details are given of what was a comparatively simple proceeding being conducted within the chamber of the authentic site of Christ's burial, it is the more difficult to grasp why we are expressly told that 'historically and ritually there is no connection' with what we perform today. Of course we do not hold our ceremonies on the original site, nor are we engaged in rescuing the Holy Land from infidel hands. We do not have spurs put upon our heels and we are not associated with St. George, but these are not the prime elements of either ceremony. Surely it is the recognition of Christ's death and resurrection by proximity to 'a sepulchre', our dedication as knights in Our Lord's service and our duties no less to both our companions and the community in which we live that are the abiding strands which link us with this recorded past. This older form may not be our Masonic Order's point of origin, and the words of today's ritual were obviously devised much later, but is there not a rich spiritual thread that helps us to realise the honourable antiquity, if not direct continuity, of what we now do?

That having been said, let us turn to another matter: the more mundane business of trying to discover just where the origins of our Holy Sepulchre and St. John the Evangelist degrees as Masonic practices might be found.

As previously mentioned, when the distinguished justice Right Worshipful Brother Waller Rodwell Wright became the Grand Master of the Red Cross of Palestine in 1804, he was also invested as the Grand Master of the Holy Sepulchre Orders. This confirms that there was some recognised connection between the two bodies at this time. What is also clear, however, is that from at least 1809 there is mention of the Noviciate of St. John the Evangelist as forming part of the Order of the Red Cross of Palestine. This arrangement is confirmed by the fact that when Rodwell Wright was in Malta and instituted an Order of the Red Cross there he is described as practising the Noviciate as part of those ceremonies.

That evidence then shows that the Holy Sepulchre and St. John the Evangelist degrees must go back at least to the start of the 19th century and probably the closing years of the 18th. We learn from Brother Wentworth Little that several very influential Craft Masons were admitted to the Red Cross degree in 1788 and he then added, 'About this period the Order of the Holy Sepulchre flourished, and in 1796 Lord Rancliffe, Grand Master of the Templars, was also the head of the Red Cross and other chivalric orders.' This means that we are now nearly two whole decades earlier than the period involving Brother Rodwell Wright, though now the suggestion is that at this stage a Holy Sepulchre ceremony was attached to the Knights Templar and that implies that we probably have to start looking in other directions for the earlier whereabouts of the Holy Sepulchre and St. John degrees.

Reference was also made earlier to the work of Brother George Draffen who pointed out how some Scottish Masons, having been to Cork to acquire other knightly degrees, became involved in setting up an Early Grand Encampment in Edinburgh, following the Irish model. That meant that for such an Early Grand Encampment to have assembled and authorised the degrees it promoted, those degrees must have been in existence and practised *before* 1770.

But dating the degree's origins is not quite so simple – we are looking for two degrees, not one. This is made clear by the rubrics that now talk of admission to the Holy Sepulchre as merely a 'reception' whereas that of St. John is called the

'Introduction of a Novice and Conferment of Knighthood'. Moreover, whilst they are closely linked today, it is clear from what has been said previously that this was not always the case. It is therefore quite possible that in our search they might appear separately and under other titles. The fact that prior to 1790 I have not yet found the terms 'Holy Sepulchre' and 'Novitiate of St. John' need not deter us from looking further.

Secondly, what seems certain is that the Holy Sepulchre degree depended on there being an existent Templar or Hospitaller knighthood if it was to be bestowed on candidates and so this Sepulchre Order was naturally developed subsequently to those more well-known ones. What we may therefore have to look for are degrees that follow on from the sequence of the Templars and Hospitallers.

Thirdly, we also know that whilst those seeking admission to the Red Cross of Constantine had only to be Master Masons, the candidates for the Holy Sepulchre and St. John degrees had to be Holy Royal Arch Masons. This is where we begin to appreciate the other part of the Historical Note which states that whilst 'the authors of the ritual are unknown, that of St. John the Evangelist was obviously influenced by the Royal Arch system'. The present ritual leaves us in not the slightest doubt for not only are we reminded of what only Royal Arch Masons can know but we are made aware that in the St. John's degree we are completing the true secrets of that Order.

It is in the degree of St. John that the most telling clues begin to appear. Three sentences especially claim our attention. They are:

> It is said that the Crusaders, finding themselves unable to expel the Saracens from the Holy Land, agreed with Godfrey de Bouillon to veil the mysteries of religion under emblems … The pyramids, being built upon rock, shadow forth the durability of the Christian faith … The words you have heard are traditionally the words of the Palestinian Order of St. John and not those of the Knights who remained in Europe during the Crusades, nor those adopted by the Knights who took possession of Rhodes and Malta.

Putting all these possible clues together we are surely led to only one conclusion. The origins of our present Holy Sepulchre and St. John ceremonies were two degrees that emerged from that extended Royal Arch panoply in Ireland which led to the Early Grand Encampment practices in the 1770s. Their names then were the Red Cross of Palestine, having a reference to the Holy Sepulchre Church there, and the Knight of Patmos, as related to St. John who was traditionally said to have dwelt on the island of that name. Those degrees appear in the Grand Encampment as the third and fourth grades of the full Templar system. As such they fit in after the Mediterranean Pass and the Knight of Malta degree, and thus fit naturally into the sequence by which they were acquired and practised later in England. Before the 1770s, their main themes will have existed as parts of the catechetical lectures that we know were part and parcel of the early and mid-18th century ceremonial in York and Ireland. They would not then, of course, have had a precise name or a separate identity.

Clearly at the heart of the Holy Sepulchre degree were the legendary events surrounding the finding of the Cross in Palestine and the political development of that land leading up to the Crusades. That of St. John the Evangelist centres on the part played by the Apostle in the discovery of the true Word, and when you add to this the descent into a vault to discover the Gospel of John you even more appreciate how this degree fits into the whole, and true, Masonic panorama. We have found the origins and the purpose.

Following the Path to our Knightly Roots

The Grand Conclave that was established under Thomas Dunckerley was the effective origin of Knight Templary as we in England know it today. What still remains is the question, from where and when did the idea and outline of such knightly Freemasonry arise?

As he seeks to answer this matter in his book *Brethren in Chivalry 1791-1991*, Em. Kt. Frederick Smyth says:

> Whatever may be concluded as to the origins of the degree of Knight Templar, it must be inferred that at the time [1769] when it was being worked in Massachusetts it was at that same period being practised elsewhere. In England, under the Grand Lodge of the Antients [formed in 1751], it was generally held that the Craft warrant conveyed powers to confer other degrees, such as those of Knight Templar and Rose Croix, in that sequence. The military lodges were in many cases also custodians of the chivalric degrees and it has to be remembered that the majority of these had been chartered by Ireland. (Op. cit. p.17)

It is more than likely that Dunckerley obtained his extra-Craft information from the military lodges with which he was closely associated during his time as the nominal Masonic ruler in Canada. This was in the period before his introduction of the Mark and Knight Templar practice in the Chapter of Friendship at Portsmouth.

Having been reminded of the Minute in St. Andrew's Royal Arch Chapter at Boston in 1769 which describes how William Davis (a Past Master of an Antients Lodge, No. 58, in the 14th Regiment of Foot) was 'begging to have and receive the Parts belonging to a Royal Arch Mason ... he was accordingly made by receiving the four Steps, that of an Excelt, Sup[er Excellent or the Veils], Royal Arch and Kt Templar'. There were also present three visitors from Lodge 322 (Irish) in the 29th Regiment of Foot. Since the presence of Irish chartered Lodge members is so evident and they belonged to Lodges warranted in 1759, it will be worth considering what is said in Lepper & Crossle's 1925 *History of the Grand Lodge of Ireland*. They refer to a statement by that notorious Grand Secretary of the Antients Grand Lodge Laurence Dermott who claimed in 1782 that it was in Fethard, County Tipperary, that Knight Templar Masons were first made in that land. The authors of the *History*, knowing the details of Masonry in that place, estimated that it must have been before 1764 (at least). This reference takes us back to the mid-1760s.

Whether it is possible to trace British Knight Templary back any further requires careful reconsideration. It begins with a quotation on p.13 of *Brethren in Chivalry*. We read there:

> Despite many earlier indications (including an unreliable Minute of 'The Lodge of Stirling Kilwinning' in 1743), the first unquestionable record of the admission of Royal Arch masons relates to a lodge at Fredericksburg [in] December 1753.

There are three issues arising from what is here said about the Stirling Minute which need further thought. First, on what grounds are we to believe that the Stirling Minute is 'unreliable'? Second, why does not our author tell us that in addition to there being this transcribed Minute, there is still displayed in that lodge room a contemporarily carved plate which shows an awareness of non-Craft degrees? Third, why are we not told that those degrees (in 1743 let me repeat) already include a Red Cross and Ark degree, a Knight of Malta and a 'Night Templar'? To state that the Minute referred to might be unreliable is worth considering, but when accompanied by this remarkable item of prized lodge furniture we may have to think again. For the record, let me introduce you to what Brother Hughan, the one-time very distinguished member of Quatuor Coronati Lodge, said about this Stirling plate when he saw it in 1893:

> The singular figures, and the concentric arches at the foot, are very suggestive, and, though not in my opinion older than about the middle of the last century, they are very noteworthy and quite unique.

Clearly, Brother Hughan did not think the reference to Knights Templar odd, even if it was striking, at the date of around 1743, and the plate which I have myself seen and held in that lodge room is now of obvious antiquity. This means, of course, that in some form there was knowledge of a Masonic Knight Templary in mid-Scotland by the 1740s at least.

That idea is severely questioned by Em. Kt. Smyth since he continues:

> In searching for the source or sources of the Masonic Order of the Temple we are led *inevitably* to the continent of Europe. We are in great difficulty, however, in establishing places and dates. There are tantalizing glimpses: for instance, it is said [and here he refers to Gould's History] that two lodges in Germany were, in the 1740s, conferring chivalric *titles* upon their members…

This passage puzzles me. If the evidence for the existence of Knight Templary among European Masons is so spasmodic then why are we led inevitably to Europe for the principal source of this degree? Moreover, if there was evidence of the Knight Templars in the German states in the 1740s then why could there not be such evidence also in Scotland? I was, of course, driven to Gould's volumes to see what he actually said. What he wrote about Freemasonry in Hamburg was this:

> Scarcely was the Provincial Grand Lodge established before Scots Masonry made itself felt. In 1744 Count Schmettau, who had carried the Scots degrees to Berlin, introduced them to Hamburg and erected the Scots Lodges Schmettau and Judica of which von Oberg and von Ronigk, the Masters of St. George and Absalom, became respectively the Scots Masters.

Titles there surely are, but not Masonic ones and not one reference to Knight Templary.

Another source for a possible early mention of Masonic Templars is the 'oration' given by the so-called Chevalier Andrew Ramsay in 1737 who appears to have 'connected, without historical foundation, Freemasonry with the Crusades and with the chivalric Orders which arose therein… He [Ramsay] established three degrees, viz. (1) Ecossais; (2) Novice; (3) Knight Templar, but nothing is added to support that statement'. (op. cit. p.14)

This French route, even by what little is here given us, hardly seems very fruitful. However, just in case we might be missing something vital let us look more closely at what Chevalier Ramsay actually said. I quote the relevant passage in what was Ramsay's *amended* oration, where alone the Crusades are mentioned:

> The Kings princes and lords returned from Palestine to their own lands and there established divers lodges. At the time of the last Crusades many lodges were already erected in Germany, Italy, Spain; France and from thence in Scotland.

This might seem to encourage theories of a direct connection between the Crusaders and Freemasonry but considering that the time of these lords' return was the late 13th century, any lodges would be lodges of operative stonemasons on building sites on their properties and not Lodges of Accepted Masons such as those with which we are familiar. Moreover, there is no mention here of these so named lodges being connected with Knight Templary as such. Of course it is possible that the contribution that Chevalier Ramsay made was to suggest or even underline the idea that what were already quasi-knightly practices could be given a more acceptable role by being associated with the Crusading knights' history, and to that we shall have to turn before our present journey is run. If that was the case, however, then a mention of Masonic Knight Templary by 1743 is not so strange after all.

The present Templar history tells us that the Rite of Strict Observance was introduced by using a legendary story of certain medieval Knights Templar who found asylum in Scotland after the dissolution of the Order in 1306, and these knights 'it was said, became members of the masons' guilds and so were direct ancestors of the speculative fraternity now under the Grand Lodge of Scotland'.

Quite apart from what elsewhere has been called hard evidence for such a route to the source of British Templar Masonry there are other factors that have to be accounted for if such a theory is to stand. The first is that Baron von Hund, the acknowledged founder of the Rite of Strict Observance, was by his own admission received into an Order of the Temple in Paris about 1742. It is not known whether this was a Masonic occasion, though the admission took place in the presence of the Earl of Kilmarnock who was Grand Master Mason of Scotland at that time. If this was part of Masonic practice at that date then it would more easily explain why there could have been acquaintance with Knights Templar in Scotland at exactly the same period and, even if it was not, the idea of associating Knightly Orders with

Masonry was obviously already around. It is certainly relevant to the idea that the Antients Masons in the 1750s were aware, as was said earlier, that other degrees than just those of the Craft and Royal Arch were accessible to their members.

Gould in his History suggested that British Masonic prisoners-of-war could have fraternised with their captors in Europe and have derived their knowledge of Knight Templary in that manner. What has to be remembered is that von Hund had not launched his Rite of Strict Observance until 1755 and it could well have been the end of that decade before contacts such as have been suggested were made. It is also true, as Em. Kt. Smyth points out, that 'von Hund was so successful with his Rite that it almost superseded the English-style Freemasonry which had hitherto been active in Germany' and it was to have great influence on the Continent.

No one denies that in the course of the Continental wars of the 18th century there could have been an interchange of Masonic ideas, but what is just as likely is that this was not an encounter from the one side only. Moreover, I have now to say that the view expressed by a Brother Hall-Johnson in 1940 in a booklet entitled *Templars and Hospitallers* is the one that I favour. He wrote: 'The belief, once widely held, that the Chevalier Michael Ramsey (sic) introduced the degree of Masonic Knights Templar during his visit to London … has long been refuted. Nor did the Templar Legend propagated by von Hund, in 1751 and subsequent years, make any impression on English-speaking Freemasonry.' What I therefore submit is that British military lodges, mainly affected by Irish traditions, already had their own growing practices regarding knightly Freemasonry and it was this that they would share with their Continental counterparts, including those who were members of the Strict Observance. In support of this view I shall now suggest three important matters, of which the third may be seen to be far and away the most important.

The first thing we have to note is the distinctiveness of the two separate forms of Masonic Knight Templary. Em. Kt. Smyth does in fact spell out in a useful, if summary, form the grounds on which those who sought to establish the Rite of Strict Observance took their stand. I quote:

…woven into its fabric was an assumption that the time was ripe for the Templars to reveal to the world their continued existence, and even for them to lay claim to the former properties and privileges of the Order. (Op. cit. p.14)

In addition, there was also an element, retained in the early forms of what we know as the 30th degree of the Rose Croix, which represented their desire for vengeance for the persecution that the original Templar Order suffered, and this is today still present in degrees of the Scandinavian rite and the Knights Beneficent of the Holy City. What is significant is that at no point do the Templar points just mentioned reveal themselves in mainstream British Knight Templary, thereby suggesting that its origin is from a different source and for rather a different purpose. We can now more clearly note the distinction between our Knight Templary and that of Continental origin.

The second matter that we must consider is the continuing question as to how and from where the military Lodges acquired the information that led to the Templar degrees. The answer is from old traditions of existing British working. In order to become a member of the subsequent Knightly Orders it was always considered necessary to be first a Past Master and a Royal Arch Mason. As this was, and still is, the requirement then it was essential that the traditional elements of these preliminary steps had to be preserved, albeit in catechetical or 'lecture' form. By 1730, we know there were those in the English Craft, and they were not only immigrants from Ireland but ex-members of the private Lodges that preceded the formation of the premier Grand Lodge in London and Westminster, who believed that old St. John Masonry was being wrongfully diluted or altered. It is no secret that in the 1730s there appear Lodges in London that are practising other (and they would claim 'more ancient') elements of Masonry that might otherwise be lost.

Principal among these elements were the genuine secrets of a true Master Mason, that is, the knowledge that was required of someone who was acknowledged to be a qualified architect or designer ruler of a Lodge of Accepted Masons. Subsequent to the 'new' grade of Master Mason that only had substituted secrets, several more steps were revealed, especially in some parts of London, in Ireland and the North-east of England. There thus appear the following: The Past Master, Select or Excellent degree; The Scots Master degree; The Super-Excellent and Arch degrees; The Red Cross degrees; and The Heredom of Kilwinning degrees. These are Masonic practices that developed in the period 1730-1750 and are therefore prior to any possible Continental influence of the kind mentioned earlier. This route to our roots is of a wholly British kind.

The link of Masonry with the idea of knighthood is clear even in the first premier Grand Lodge traditional history of 1722 where we read that St. Alban, 'who instructed the King in the said Science of Masonry … became in high Favour with the King, insomuch that he was Knighted…', and to underline this link and show the direction in which influence was thought to flow we have the following passage in the 1723 Constitutions:

'from this ancient Fraternity the Societies or Orders of the Warlike Knights, and of the Religious too, in process of time did borrow many solemn Usages: for none were better instituted than the accepted Masons…'. (Spencer edn. 1871 pp.58-60)

From 1730 we know that there were 'Masters Lodges' where the new 3rd degree was to be conferred but in which there was seated a superior group called Scots (or Ecossais) Masters, who always had their place in the East, wore hats, as was the custom with Installed Masters, had swords, a sash and a distinctive decoration, and claimed knowledge of the genuine secrets of a true Master Mason. In a French exposure of the Ecossais Master degree printed in 1744, but clearly well established by then, we have the following catechism:

Q. Are you an Ecossais Master?
A. I was brought out of the captivity of Babylon.
Q. Who honoured you with the degree of Ecossais?
A. Prince Zerubbabel, of the line of David and Solomon…
Q. In what are the Ecossais Masons occupied?
A. In rebuilding the Temple of God.
Q. Why do the Ecossais Masons carry the sword and buckler (or shield)?
A. In memory of the order given to all workmen at the time of the rebuilding of the Temple, to have swords always at their sides and their bucklers near at hand, for use in case of attack by their enemies.

So here we have not only what are recognisable Royal Arch features but what are evidently warrior Masons closely associated with the building of a Temple.

We also know that in central London from about 1735 there were lodges working a 'Heredom of Kilwinning' ritual that has changed very little up to the present day. For any who are not members of that tradition, that was later discontinued in England but was adopted north of the border and called The Royal Order of Scotland, the following quote may come as a pleasant surprise because it contains ritual that was to become very familiar to any Knight Templar. I quote:

You promise now in manner most sincere,
In presence of that God we all revere,
And of these Knights and brethren of the Art
Who unto you their Secrets may impart,
That you will always keep, guard and conceal..
And that under a penalty no less severe
Than that your head from body we may tear
And on that Tower grand affix the same…

And was this latter action not the old Knight Templar penal sign? The ceremony takes place in the context of the eventual rebuilding of the Second Temple at Jerusalem and the formal admission of the candidate in a Provincial Lodge or Council. Part of the lecture, still in its ancient verse form, is this:

On bended knee I there was placed…
While Knights did round me stand…
I eke three strokes on back received
With Sword; upreared at last,
A Sign and Token, each of which
Did form a Cross complete;
A Word also I did receive
So soon as on my feet…

The Word so communicated is exactly the same as the Knight Templar of today is privy to. All this then in a Masonic form of English knighthood by 1740.

What has also to be noted is that when in the 1740s there is a practice of what was to be the Royal Arch and some knightly degrees, in the new military lodges and other lodges influenced by them, both the Scots Masters and the English Heredom Order disappear completely from the scene. The Knight Templars are beginning to evolve, not only in Stirling but elsewhere, and the Order's strong traditional link with the Holy Royal Arch is fixed.

This is confirmed because we know that by 1740 in both York and Ireland there was a legend concerning the discovery of the Sacred Law in the foundations of the Temple in King Josiah's time, as well as a Zerubbabel one, and in Ireland the events in and after leaving Babylon are described in various 'Red Cross Knight' degrees. So again the close ties with the Royal Arch are demonstrated.

In 1748 a book was published in Dublin entitled *Masonry, the Turnpike Road to Happiness in this life*. On page 29 comes this passage: 'Descending into more modern times I might enumerate among our members the Knights Hospitallers of Jerusalem and all the illustrious lords who distinguished themselves in the Crusades.' Already, it would seem that the idea of associating these knightly bodies with those who practised the Free and Accepted Craft had surfaced. With such ideas already in circulation is it any wonder that even before the Antient Masons appear on the English scene officially in 1751, there are Irish-warranted military lodges who have not only begun to carry out knightly degrees but are prepared to describe two of them as Knight Templar and Knight of Malta. By the 1770s, they even had a Knighthood of St. Paul which was to be the foundation of what we now call the Mediterranean Pass. Of course, this is not to say that the form or content of these 'degrees' was identical with what we practise today. All that we need to know is that from our native British soil the seeds were early enough sown from which our main Masonic knight ceremonies would take hold.

When, How and Where Did the
Knight Templar Priests Begin?

Keith Jackson tells us in *Beyond the Craft* that this degree 'has its foundations in Ireland where records exist of workings in the late 1700s'. While this is true, the definitive origin is still a mystery.

The first difficulty to be faced is that previously this degree was apparently worked under such titles as the Priestly Order of the Temple, the White Masons, the Christian Order of Melchizedek or the Ne Plus Ultra. To give a flavour of what would have been around in the late 1770s let us look at some of the rites that are named above. The first is the 'Priestly Order of the Temple', otherwise known as the White Masons. This ceremony opened with all present robed in the white dress of the Templars and in a tabernacle 'that was perfect and not made with hands'. Those who served here were a holy priesthood offering up 'spiritual sacrifices acceptable to God by Jesus Christ' and A.E. Waite's description continues:

> The Candidate enters carrying the titles of peace, faith and goodwill. He is welcomed in the Name of the King of Peace, the Eternal Melchizedek. He passes successively (and symbolically) through 7 mystical doors; through that of Faith, uplifting the Lamp of Prayer; of Hope, with the Lamp of Knowledge; of Mercy, having the Lamp of Desire; of Utterance, with the Lamp of Purity; of Salvation, upholding a Lamp of Good Works; of Penance, with a Lamp of Power and finally through a Door of Life – meaning the Life of life – carrying a Lamp of Joy, as of those who come into their own. So he is led to the East to be anointed with oil in the name of the Lord and consecrated a Priest Mason. Thereafter these Templar Priests resolve together … to unite their souls in the Lord's path that they may become spiritual builders and pillars in the House of God ... by the all-sufficient grace and spirit of God. (The New Encyclopaedia Vol.II p.294)

There were also seven Passwords, seven Manners of Refreshment and seven Seals. In the light of that information from Waite it seems most likely that this was an earlier version of the Knight Templar Priest and not least as it is attached to the year 1686 as a date for the revival of this degree. We shall return to this date and its significance later in this chapter.

What is equally intriguing in the mention of this degree as part of the Scottish Grand Council of Rites was that the very next degree in their series was 'The Priest of the Sun'. Here we have 7 subordinate officers corresponding to 7 angels who preside over the 7 planets of the ancients. The candidate is guided by a Conductor called Truth who takes him in turn from angel to angel. The order of introductions and encounters is as follows:

1. As a Master Mason to Michael, representing the sun, the candidate is counselled to remember that the Kingdom of Heaven belongs to the poor in spirit;
2. As a Royal Arch Mason to Gabriel, representing the moon, who reminds the Mason that comfort is for those who mourn; (It may be of interest at this point to note that the reason why the sun and moon in medieval times always have faces is because they represented Michael and Gabriel.)
3. As a Knight Templar to Uriel, representing Mercury, who announces that the meek shall inherit the earth;
4. As a Prince Mason to Hamaliel, representing the governing of Venus, who speaks of the blessing promised to those who hunger and thirst after righteousness;
5. As a Knight of St. Andrew to Raphael, the ruler of Mars, who affirms that the merciful will obtain mercy;
6. As a Knight Kadosh to Zarachiel, the angel of Jupiter, who declares that the pure in heart shall see God;
7. As a Knight Templar Priest to Saphael, president of Saturn, who recalls for the candidate that peacemakers are the Children of God.

The candidate is then pledged and proclaimed by Father Adam. Whilst Brother Waite considers this proceeding to be 'Pure nonsense' it has to be acknowledged that the seven-point introduction and instruction procedure, the ranks of Masonic attainment required, the Christian beatitudes imparted and the evident recognition of Knight Templar Priests surely strike significant chords for all priestly

Masons. Could it even be that some of the features of the second of these degrees were incorporated into the former to create something even nearer to what we know today?

The other example of contemporary working at that time was one called 'Ne Plus Ultra'. I quote from a handwritten copy of the Early Grand Encampments:

The following ritual is that adopted by the Royal Kent Tabernacle at Newcastle on Tyne. On the altar is a triangular sconce containing 12 lights with a cross in between ... A pyramidal figure with 4 triangular sides is suspended by a black cord over the altar and on the sides are the words, 'Glory be to God on high', 'Peace on Earth' and 'Goodwill towards men'. The Book of the Sacred Law is placed in front of the sconce.

The copy then continues:

The member knights enter clothed in white mantles with a red cross on their left breast. The candidates are then marshalled and march in and are seated in the West. They then listen to Exodus 20 and Leviticus 19 as their laws and then Matthew 5, vv. 1-13, the Sermon on the Mount as their blessings. They then take an obligation in which the penalty is that of being deprived of the True Word and they then seal the declaration nine times. They then form triangles and exchange three times the names of the Holy Trinity. They then partake of bread and wine, hear the final chapter of the Book of Revelation read, and are then presented with the collection box for charity. Thereafter, if there is no other business, the Conclave is closed but not before the Senior Warden has communicated some 'scientific instruction' to the junior brethren.

Whilst there are obvious similarities between some of the dress, the readings and the furniture with what Knight Templar Priests encounter today, there cannot be any doubt that this is not a predecessor of the present degree. This is because at the end of the list of the degrees conferred in the Tabernacle in 1809 it states clearly, after the very same list of further degrees that are now communicated to Knight Priests, these titles: Holy Royal Arch Knight Templar Priest, or Order of Holy Wisdom, and then, Grand High Priest of the Tabernacle, or the Templars' Ne Plus Ultra.

Therefore, by that date there was a clearly defined and separate degree of Knight Templar Priest and as is certainly the case now, it was this that completed all future proceedings of the Order, not the Ne Plus Ultra which belonged to the Knights Templar practice. It is worth noting that in fact that final 'degree' did not persist as a part of the parent knightly body.

In any case, the authors of the new history of this order tell us that the first firm evidence of the establishment of a Union Band is confirmed by the constitution of such a body in Anahilt in County Down, Northern Ireland, on 8 November 1792. Even as they record this fact, however, they also state that there may well have been earlier Bands because Anahilt is not numbered No.1. Moreover, the next two Bands, in 1799, were numbered No.4 at Banbridge and No.5 at Dromore. Both these villages are in the same area of the Ulster Province. All this serves to narrow down the period of the Order's emergence since it seems clear that it must have been after the likely development of the Knight Templar Order in Ireland which is now agreed as being around 1760, and the emergence of these Bands around 1790.

The authors provide several other clues:

...it is felt that there must be a connection with the Holy Order of Wisdom somewhere waiting to be discovered. It is probably too simplistic to suggest that the alternative title was inspired by the theme of the Order, from Proverbs IX (v.)

1: 'Wisdom hath builded her house, she hath hewn out seven pillars.'

The suggestion about there being some connection with an Order of Wisdom is almost certainly correct, and this is made even more likely when we learn that a very similar degree to the White Masons mentioned above is, in the rite named 'The Initiated Brothers of Asia', immediately preceded by 'The Masters of the Wise or of Wisdom'. Further searching may still be necessary, but such a connection with the Wisdom notion is beginning to be more evident.

We should also note a quote by the new history's authors from a mid-19th century ritual that may have come from Scotland. Here we read:

...some suppose it was a degree given to Commanders only, or the Chaplains, the Templar degree usually being given [to] the Military, this the Religious part of the Ritual. But if the Chaplains alone obtained it, they must have gone through the military portion first, as the present is a mere appendage to it. Others suppose that the Knights were at first admitted as warriors, but having served it with honour they were consecrated and hence this portion of the ceremony is presided over by a Prelate or High Priest, and this was the original view in forming this Masonic degree. It is well known in some parts of Ireland [such as Belfast] and Scotland but is scarcely so known in England, at least at the present day.

We have here a very significant reflection on this degree at a period when its practice and development had been very active and within a century of its inauguration. What has to accompany this reflection is the most useful map showing the distribution in County Down of the Union Bands in which a Knight Priest Order mostly occurred. This is where the main body of Protestant settlers of the 17th century, both those from Scotland and Huguenots from France, were allocated land and where, from that time onwards, devotion to three major factors was paramount. The factors were a steadfast and patriotic allegiance to the British Crown, a deep and informed respect for the Holy Bible, and a cultivated and unshakeable attachment to the Reformed religion, which was not least represented by the Established Church. Nor is that all.

The authors of our new history remind readers that in 1686, on the eve of the last revolution to take place on British soil, a body of seven Bishops, or should we not rather say *Prelates*, were commemorated by a medal being struck in their honour. The Bishops in question, led by Dr. Sancroft, the Archbishop of Canterbury, had protested against the idea that it was lawful for anyone to reject the person and authority of a consecrated monarch, in this case King James II, even though he was not a member of the Established Church. They felt that the principle of obedience to the British monarch was so essential that they were even willing to forgo freedom and the exercise of their important offices. Because they would not swear allegiance to Queen Anne, James II's daughter, and King William, who were invited to the throne as joint Protestant rulers, the Bishops were ever after known as the non-Jurors.

The medal that was struck to commemorate this historic protest was inscribed on one side with: 'Wisdom hath builded her House. She hath hewn out her Seven Pillars.' On the other was inscribed: 'The Gates of Hell shall not prevail.' The words on the first side, from Proverbs, were those adopted as the text of this Order from its earliest days and also appear in its ritual to this day.

The year 1686 was significant for another reason. It was the year following the revoking, or cancellation, of the Edict of Nantes that had guaranteed the right of the Huguenots and other Protestants in France to exercise their vote and their religion. In 1686, there began the exodus of some half a million Frenchmen to England and Ireland, and a substantial number of these immigrants, skilled in weaving, settled in the area around a town called Lisburn, just to the east of Belfast, where flax had soil conditions most suitable for its growth. Here then was another section of a community that shared the religious convictions of its neighbours and a profound sense of gratitude to the British Crown for the chance of new homes and a livelihood.

It should not therefore surprise us that the Masonic writer John Yarker, who came from a 19th century Manchester in which the impact of Irish immigration was then powerfully felt, should start to make a connection between 1686 and what had now been the growth of Union Bands, with the Knight Priestly degree, in the towns just around and to the north of the city. He, in his 1869 'Notes on the Orders of the Temple and St. John and the Jerusalem Encampment Manchester' states that 1686 in an 1813 ritual was declared to be the 'year of the revival', adding: 'It is quite possible that the degree may have been designed at this period of revival as a Protestant Order, and a test among the Knights Templar.'

It may be, as the new authors rightly point out, that though the Priesthood was certainly instituted as a Protestant Order it could not have been in 1686. The connection with that date is very understandable, however, and what now becomes a real and acceptable alternative is that 1786 becomes the year for the revival of the ideas that were so powerfully generated a century earlier and hence the time for launching as an entirely separate and authentic practice what hitherto may have been, for perhaps a decade, a side degree, or even just an historical adjunct to the developing Knight Templar degree – the affirmation of those patriotic, biblical and religious convictions that were so fitting in the heart of Protestant Ulster. Is it even conceivable that, recognising the strong historical links of the Knights Templar and Malta Knights with the Roman Catholic Church and the continuing attendance of Irish Roman Catholic Masons up to the mid-19th century, in some parts of Ireland there should be an additional ceremony and obligation, based entirely on biblical texts, that would reassure some brethren of the political and religious status of their members.

The authors of the new history have given us material to support this view by quoting from an early ritual on p.11 which reads as follows:

'Beloved Brethren, always look into the perfect Law & Liberty and receive with meekness the ungrafted word which is able to save your souls. A Royal Arch Knight Templar Priest assents to all the principles of TRUE RELIGION which are agreeable to the Holy Scriptures and Right Reason and believes all the articles of religion which God as [sic] revealed to us by his Son.' Nor is this all. The By-laws reveal an undeniable trend in a Protestant, community and patriotic direction:

'Every Member of this sacred order shall bring with him the OULD & NEW TESTAMENT & meet together in some convenient place as the members shall think proper … to Instruct and Edify each other up in Faith and Holiness. You must not carry on, or know to be carried on, any secret plot Against the Brotherhood, our Country or our King so long as he and the Male heir Aparent [sic] to the Crown shall continue true to their Coronation Oath, but will freely give timely notice as ye friends of all approaching dangers as far as your severall knowledge leads you.'

By no stretch of the imagination could any devout member of the Roman Catholic Church subscribe to such ardently biblical and evangelical sentiments, together with the devotion to an avowedly Protestant monarchy. One may dare to say here that faced with the precepts of the early Holy Royal Arch Knight Templar Priests it is not hard to see from where the next stage, that of the Orange Order, emerged. Only our general principle of not introducing political or religious topics into our Lodge meetings can have saved most of us from that further progress.

It would seem then that we are rather nearer to the goal we have been seeking as to when this Order began and developed into the Order which we know. Brought already through the warrior companionship of building a second Temple and endued with the knightly qualities of Christians who took the Temple's name or followed in the steps of St. John the Hospitaller of Jerusalem, our Irish brethren in the North-east of Ireland recalled their history and sought a way in which they might ensure that traditions of belief and practice would not be lost. By the 1770s, there were some Masons who wanted to test the Brotherhood by one more knightly gesture. In one lodge or another experiments of catechisms or declarations based on scriptural knowledge were no doubt being tried and then, at last, there was a pattern of seven avowals for the brethren towards one another:

First to keep his secrets
Second to assist him in all his needs
Third to Counsil [sic] him when he wants Advice
Fourth to Cheer when he wants Comfort
Fifth to endeavour to Relieve him out of troubles & dangers
Sixth to Aid [and] Assist his Soul in all spiritual Wants
Seventh it is their duty to be always Faithful to Each other.

And so the seven pillars of the 1686 memorial are born. By 1786, the first distinct forms of the degree could be practised as a true revival of 1686 events and principles, and by 1792 in Anahilt, someone has the idea of recording and preserving the fact that this Order was at work.

I cannot resist the moving words of an Irish Mason, Right Worshipful Brother Samuel Leighton, in 1932, when he said:

Stern puritanical admonitions were administered to the members as to the mode of conduct to each other in their everyday life. The old Pillar Priest may, to some, be a sort of joke, but those men in the simplicity of their lives, in the toil of the country farmer's occupation were inculcating the noblest principles of character, and their memory is worthy of our highest respect and admiration. (Op. cit. p.12)

It only remains to say a word about the appendant degrees attached to this Order. The authors of the *Priestly Order* tell us that in 1893:

...members of the Order applied, presumably with the consent of the Knights Grand Cross, for a warrant to work as Royal Kent Council [in Newcastle upon Tyne] ... It was at this point that Matier endeavoured to ensure that the other degrees (which, of course, included The Order of Knight Templar Priests) being worked at Newcastle were incorporated in the Allied Masonic Degrees'. (Op. cit. p.42)

This remained the arrangement until 1924 when a Grand College was separately established and the list of 31 intermediate degrees was transferred to its care and control. This arrangement has persisted ever since. There is no space here to explain in detail from where the individual degrees conferred by name upon candidates are derived, but we have a handbook by G.E.W. Bridge which serves that purpose. It is essential reading for admitted members of the Holy Royal Arch Knight Templar Priests.

A Further Reading List

The Arch and the Rainbow. Revd. Neville B. Cryer.

The Mark Degree. David Mitchell. Lewis Masonic, 2003.

History of the Order of the Secret Monitor. R.J. Wilkinson. Grand Council, London, 1964.

The Cryptic Rite: an Historical Treatise. R.J. Wilkinson. Grand Council, London, 1977.

The Order of the Allied Masonic Degrees. Harold Prestige, with Second Edition by Frederick Smyth. London, 1999.

Rose Croix. Brig. A.C.F. Jackson. Lewis Masonic, 1980.

Ancient and Accepted. John Mandleberg. QCCC Ltd, 2000.

Rose Croix Essays. John Mandleberg. Lewis Masonic, 2005.

The History and Origin of the Masonic and Military Order of the Red Cross of Constantine. Anon. London, 1981.

Brethren in Chivalry 1791-1991. Frederick Smyth. Lewis Masonic, 1991.

The Priestly Order: The History of the Order of the Holy Royal Arch Knight Templar Priests. R. Cooley & M. Knowles. Grand College Ltd, 2006.